THE LORDS OF THE SAVANNAH

Leopards &
Cheetahs

TEXT AND PHOTOGRAPHS
CHRISTINE AND MICHEL DENIS-HUOT

HISTORICAL INTRODUCTION
GIANNI GUADALUPI

EDITORIAL DIRECTOR
VALERIA MANFERTO DE FABIANIS

GRAPHIC DESIGN
PATRIZIA BALOCCO LOVISETTI

GRAPHIC
MARIA CUCCHI

CONTENTS

1
Always on the alert, the female cheetah raises her cubs on her own.

2-3
Leopards, resting on a tree branch for hours, mostly settle in inconspicuous spots.

4-5
A young female cheetah improves her running speed by chasing unattainable prey.

6-7
Cheetah cubs practice hunting at the expense of a newborn gazelle.

8
Having made the kill, a female cheetah checks her surroundings.

9
Leopards can be individually identified by the spots on their face.

10-11
Five-week-old leopards wait for their mother to return from hunting.

12-13
Reawakening in the savanna: a female leopard and her cub wait for the sun to "perce la brume" and warm them.

© 2006 White Star S.p.A.
Via Candido Sassone, 22/24
13100 Vercelli, Italy
www.whitestar.it

Translation
Timothy Stroud
Amy Ezrin

ISBN 88-544-0089-0

REPRINTS:
1 2 3 4 5 6   10 09 08 07 06

Printed in Thailand
Color separation by Fotomec, Turin

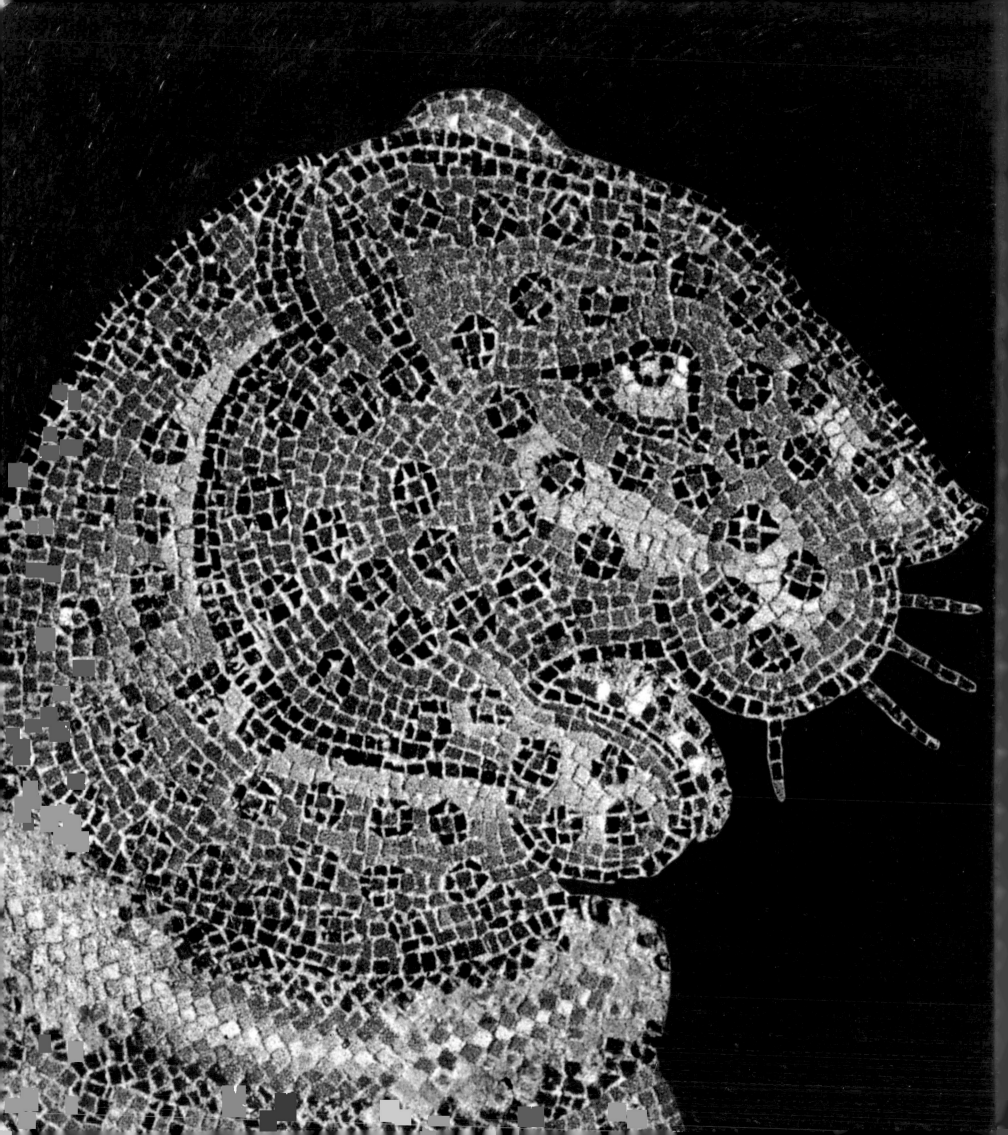

THE TIME OF THE PARDS

14

The head of this leopard, featured in the Triumph of Bacchus and Arianna. This 3rd-century-A.D. floor mosaic found in the house of Liber Pater, in Libya, expresses majesty more than ferocity.

15

Indifferent to the abundant prey surrounding them, the two leopards shown in this 17th-century painting from the school of Ferdinand van Kessel romp like peaceful kittens: in fact, they are in the Garden of Eden, from which all cruelty has been banned.

16

Having secured his meal, this leopard painted by Daniel Girand Elliot between 1860 and 1877, looks around with arrogant anxiousness, while the unharmed monkeys behind his back restrain their anger.

17

The 19th century's zest for geographical exploration led to the rise of the zoo and the growth of enthusiasm for natural history. The leopard became one of the favorite subjects of painters like Jacques-Laurent Agasse (1787-1849), who made this painting.

The zoologists of Antiquity believed that the leopard (*leo-pardus*) was the result of an impure mating between a luxurious lioness and a *pard*, a word that indicated the male panther. The lion learned of this reproachable union by repeatedly sniffing his unfaithful consort, taking his revenge on her by slashing her with his fangs and claws. For this reason, the sinful lioness, once the deed was done, ran to wash herself in a river, and for a while did not go near her husband, but followed him at a distance.

The *pard* exuded a particularly sharp but sweet odor, and he used this extraordinary quality of his to attract the other animals, seize them, and claw them up. However, to be successful in this deception, he had to keep his head hidden, or its particularly ferocious appearance would have frightened his victim who, before falling into his clutches, would have taken off.

The fruit of a hybrid and adulterous love, the leopard could never be famous in a positive light. They are cruel and capricious, said the naturalists of the 16th century, citing Greek and Roman fables: "Leopards have a great desire to rip animals apart in order to suck their blood; they live in groups along rivers or in areas covered by trees or bushes, they greedily enjoy wine, and they often get drunk, thus falling victim to man."

These alcoholic beasts sometimes devour each other "and when they are sated, go rest in their dens until their digestion is complete. If they swallow poisonous herbs, they save themselves by devouring a bit of human excrement, which acts as an antidote."

Conrad Gesner, one of the 16th century's greatest scholars of natural history, cited a story told by the sophist Claudius Aelianus, who lived in Rome in the 3rd century AD, according to which leopards were highly skilled at catching monkeys. "They lie down on the ground, stretch out their paws, cover their eyes, and hold their breath, pretending to be dead. The monkeys, satisfied that their enemy has met its end, approach. Some of the more daring, after a bit of hesitation, will bend towards the snout of the leopard to better observe its eyes and mouth to be absolutely certain it is no longer breathing. The leopard will continue to play dead. All the monkeys, totally certain, then start to sneer and jeer at it. The leopard will wait until they are tired then pounce upon them and kill a large number of them, taking the biggest and fattest for his meal."

18-19

In the 19th century, European publishers issued sumptuous illustrated volumes dedicated to the animals of the world, with color panels that were often true works of art. Here, an anonymous but talented artist enchants readers with a depiction of the leopard cubs' gentle aspect and their mother's affectionate nature.

19 top

On the other hand, another 19th-century artist concentrates on the leopard's ferocity, associating the beast with a shaggy hyena and an indifferent Bengal jackal intent on sniffing a bone. The precision with which the artist has drawn the three different animals is remarkable.

19 bottom

This captured leopard, the work of Japanese artist Kawanabe Kyosai (1831-1889), who captions his illustration "Savage tiger, never seen before," roars in annoyance at the almost mocking presence of a rooster free to fly around as it pleases.

Gesner proceeded to collect other legends passed down from classical-era texts. "The leopard rarely gives birth and only to one cub at a time; labor is accompanied and followed by terrible suffering." Sometimes, the leopard breeds with a wolf, and a hybrid is born called *theos*, with a spotted coat and a head just like that of wolves. Whereas the lion can be compared with a fair and noble man, the leopard can be associated with a shrewd and mean woman. Leopards demonstrate great affection for their cubs, about which Demetrius tells the following story: a man once met a leopard that, instead of attacking him, started to rub up against his legs. At first, the man was afraid, but then believed that the animal was trying to invite him to follow it, and reassured, did what it wanted. The leopard then led him near a deep ditch into which his little ones had fallen. The man saved them, and the leopard did everything possible to show his gratitude. There was also a leopard that refused to eat the meat of a little goat with which he was raised.

The leopard is much hated by men, who run from him as if he were a dragon, and it in turn hates men so much that it will destroy their effigies. It also hates roosters and snakes. Like the lion, it withdraws its claws when walking so as to not wear them down and render them too dull to slash its enemies during struggles. Leopards are afraid of hyenas, to the point that when they see them, they lose their strength. Pliny claims that if two were to attack each other, one wearing the skin of a leopard and one the hide of a hyena, the former would lose all its hair. For this reason, when the Ancient Egyptians wanted to show that a vile being can be victorious over a valiant one, they would paint one with the hide of a hyena and one with the skin of a leopard."

The denigration of this poor beast lasted for a long time; in 1873, the entry about the leopard in the Larousse *Grand Encyclopedia* still expressed conclusions bordering on insulting: it was not only ferocious and wild, as would befit a wild beast, but also "little accommodating, irritable, and deceitful," not to mention "wicked and bloodthirsty."

Only the Christian medieval era was a bit fairer to that which was called *pard* or panther. In animal books, it only knew one enemy, the dragon. "When it eats to satisfaction, it seeks refuge in its den and falls asleep. After three days, it wakes up, makes a big roar, and emits a sweet-smelling breath like a mixture of many aromas from its mouth. Hearing the roar of the panther, the other animals follow it anywhere it goes, attracted by such fragrant sweetness. Only the dragon, terrified by its voice, flees to underground caves where, out of the range of the panther's exhalation, it falls asleep and remains as immobile as the dead." The panther or *pard* personifies Jesus Christ, "who took the power from the dragon that symbolized the demon," its numerous spots representing the infinite virtues of the Savior, omnipotent, all-knowing, and all-seeing.

Medieval heraldry also assigned the leopard a role inspiring the utmost respect: it represents "those gifted and generous warriors that have performed some daring act with strength, courage, readiness, and agility." In France, the image of the leopard was emblazoned on the coat of arms of those that reported victories over the English, as it was considered to symbolize England.

The leopard enjoyed even greater favor among various African tribes, who preferred it over the lion as an animal emblematic of royalty. In the kingdom of Dahomey, for example, the appearance of the sovereign was saluted by the unanimous cry of "Here comes the leopard!" from his subjects. When he was not wearing the multicolored robes sold to him by European merchants, that monarch wrapped his hips in leopard skins, which also lined his wooden throne. The skins were considered to hold great value and were the source of great business (which lasted centuries and led to the slaughter of half the leopard population).

Other chieftains – the most powerful, the most respected – kept an enclosure in their realms for captured felines, and in some cases, when they were able to domesticate them, they had the cats lie down next to them at public hearings.

20
This leopard, portrayed in a tapestry at the Wawel Castle in Cracow, the old capital of the Kingdom of Poland, has a rather mythical appearance, almost as much as the dragon sinking its teeth into the cat.

21
Leopard skins, like the lion's mane, were symbolic of strength and valor for many African tribes. In this 1849 lithograph by George French Angas, some Zulu warriors wear them like helmets, finishing off the headdress with ostrich feathers.

The cheetah could be easily domesticated, exploited since the most remote ancient times as a hunting aid. It seems to have been the Ancient Egyptians to first use them in this way, but this kind of hunting art, as highly considered as that of falconry, was also practiced in India, Persia, and Mongolia. In the Persian Empire, from the Achaemenids until the beginning of the last century, the most important lords had entire packs of perfectly trained cheetahs, with numerous servants dedicated to their upkeep. This was also the case in the India of the rajas, where the fastest, most skillful, and most aggressive cheetahs were worth their weight in gold. It seems, however, that the Mughals had the most strongly burning passion for cheetahs. There were those that kept up to a thousand of them, spending fabulous amounts to maintain them and continually import new ones from every part of the continent.

Some European sovereigns also wanted to try this exotic hunting method. Emperor Leopld I, ruler of the Holy Roman Empire from 1658 to 1705, for example, received a gift of two cheetahs that he keep with his hunting dogs, which loved each other and got along well, and which he used often.

Hunting with cheetahs normally took place on horseback: the feline sat comfortably in the saddle behind the knight, chained and blindfolded. The group ventured deep into the valleys where gazelles usually grazed. When the hunter spotted one, he stopped, undid the beast's blindfold, and pointed in the direction it was supposed to attack. The cheetah slipped down from the saddle and, without making any noise, slid behind the bushes, through the tall grass and rocks, taking advantage of any features of the terrain. Finally, having reached an opportune distance without being seen, with two or three prodigious leaps, it fell with incredible speed on its prey, and after having killed it, sucked its blood. The cheetah's owner, who would have been watching this unfair fight from afar, came at a gallop and compensated the animal with abundant petting and a measure of the victim's blood. Sometimes, the gazelle might have been able to escape, perhaps being prematurely alerted by a clumsy move on the part of its pursuer. Witnesses recount that in this case the unsuccessful predator would show a form of shame over the unfortunate event, and it would take much flattery from the hunter to console it and make it resume the hunt for a second opportunity.

22 top
Hunting with cheetahs and falcons has been practiced throughout Asia for many centuries. In this early-17th-century Mogul miniature, the feline is entrusted to the care of a falconer.

22 bottom
As a servant removes the blindfold, his Indian companion points out to the cheetah the deer in the background. The picture is by the English painter George Stubbs (1724-1806).

23
Dressed as Melchior, Giuliano de' Medici rides in the Procession of the Three Kings by Benozzo Gozzoli with a cheetah in the saddle next to him. To the side, an attendant is about to get another cheetah to jump onto his horse's back by pulling its leash.

In India, rulers used to go hunting with many cheetahs carried on a special cart. They believed that the antelopes and gazelles allowed themselves to be approached more easily by a vehicle than a group of people.

Accidents could happen, especially if the predators were not perfectly trained. Sometimes, cheetahs did not pounce on the game but rather on the dogs of the pack that were part of the hunt, or they attacked flocks of sheep and goats grazing in the area. They were still rare cases, because these felines distinguished themselves by their intelligence as much as their mildness. Nonetheless, even if domesticated, they could not stand to be shut up in cramped spaces. Those that were held in the cages of zoos often got sick and died at the end of a year or so, whereas they lived until a ripe old age if they had large spaces in which to roam. However, cheetahs have been known to grow accustomed to living in houses, behaving exactly like dogs. They wandered from one room to another, dozed curled up in corners, ate from a bowl, and rubbed up against their owner's legs and licked their hands.

Chained in an enclosure that is more symbolic than real, tied to an odd pointed object, the cheetah painted by Giovannino de' Grassi in his journal belongs to heraldry as much as to zoology.

24-25
This hunting leopard, depicted in an Indian miniature painted in Seringapatam between 1798 and 1805, seems to display his spotted coat as if he were pleased with himself.

25 top
This hunter's ox-drawn wagon has come close to wild game; the cheetah is about to be liberated so that he can pounce on the prey.

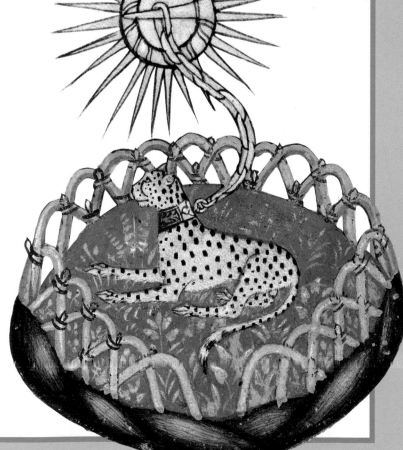

26

*Leaping from a tree in which
he has been waiting in
ambush, this Art-Deco leopard
sinks his teeth into a gazelle.
This painting, completed in
1931 by Louis Bouquet, hangs
in the Musée des Arts
d'Afrique et d'Océanie,
in Paris.*

27

*Involved in a unique
conversation made up of roars,
a curly-haired lion and an
overly snub-nosed leopard wag
their tails in this
Flemish-school tapestry
woven around 1551.*

Although cheetahs can become as lovable as cats, leopards seem to be much more fearsome. Africans were convinced that it was one of the most expert felines at attacking men. They actually believed that they especially loved human flesh. According to some tribes, however, man-eating leopards were none other than men, assuming the appearance of beasts by magic.

Legend has it that once upon a time a man and wife were returning from the market when, crossing the forest, they saw a giant leopard. The woman, terrorized, wanted to flee, but the man calmed her down by revealing a secret: he had a powder, and if he swallowed it, he, too, would have been able to transform himself into a leopard stronger than real ones and able to make the giant run away. He pulled out the magic substance, swallowing half and giving the rest to his wife, advising her to give it back to him once the leopard had escaped. Within seconds, he changed into a fanged and clawed beast, and with a tremendous roar, leapt onto his peer, which seeing itself attacked, disappeared into the jungle. However, not only the leopard vanished: the woman, seeing that the carnivores had become two, was gripped by such irrational fear that, forgetting the one beast to be her husband in disguise, started to run like a madwoman and dropped the powder. Her consort, forced to remain a leopard for the rest of his life, got so angry that he caught up with her, killed her, and ate her. He did not stop with her: since then, and for many years

thereafter, he remained the most terrifying man-eating beast in the entire region.

At the origin of this and other similar stories is the leopard-men sect, one of the many secret African societies whose members wore the skins of their totem animals, even using weapons made with claws to kill their victims, so that they would appear to have been ripped apart by a leopard. However, in many African tales, more than feared for its ferocity, this feline is praised for its majesty, to the point that it often replaces the lion as king of the jungle. Like the lion, it is often mocked by smaller, harmless beasts like the hare, the tortoise, and the gazelle. One Congolese fable tells the story of Leopard and Gazelle that were farming a field together, but the astute herbivore was always claiming to be sick so that the carnivore would have to do all the work. In the end, when Gazelle went to see the plantation at harvest time, she found it so abundant that she invited all the antelopes and every other animal she met to a banquet. The next day, Leopard came and discovered that everything had been devoured. He then placed traps to catch the thieves. Of course, a careless antelope fell in one, and when Leopard found it, he ate it. However, gazelle, upon hearing this fact, wanted to vindicate her friend. She made a drum and began to beat it to call the animals to a big ball. Leopard heard it too, and, under assault and outnumbered, was killed. This fairy-tale settling of scores by ruminants with their devourers could only be possible in the world of fantasy.

ENVIRONMENT AND ANATOMY

28
A female cheetah (left) and a female leopard (right): the two spotted felines scan the surrounding plains in search of prey.

30
The spots of leopards, clustered in rosettes on the bank and flanks, give way to simple dots on the head, neck, and paws.

31
On the cheetah's snout, two magnificent black tear tracks descend toward the juncture of the lips.

Cheetahs and leopards belong to the order of Carnivores, within which they are members of the family of Felines; and within this family cheetahs *(Acinonyx jubatus)* form their own subfamily. Leopards *(Panthera pardus)* are members of the Panthera subfamily of large cats with tigers, jaguars and lions. The connection between the four large felines seems to be the presence of an elastic ligament in the hyoid arch in the throat, a series of small bones that provide support to the vocal chords and tongue. The third sub-family of Felines is formed by the "small cats," like the lynx, puma, serval, and domestic cat.

However, for many years the classification of the various species of felines has undergone modification following DNA research that has thrown new light onto their family tree. Rather than compare their physical characteristics, as used to happen, now experts prefer to study the animals' genetic differences, as identical physical characteristics can exist in species that have no relationship to one another at all. The new studies on genetics have suggested that cheetahs belong to the same evolutionary line as the puma and jaguarundis, a small cat South American cat.

Science has shown that felines have existed for at least 30 million years, in other words, since 35 million years after the extinction of the dinosaurs. It is not clear what their origins were, though it seems that their first "modern" form was *Proailurus* in Europe, of which fossils have been discovered in France. *Proailurus* weighed about 22 pounds and probably spent much of its time in the trees. Ten million years later *Pseudæleurus* appeared, the ancestor of both the small and large cats of today and of the saber-toothed tigers that lived during the Miocene period 10 to 15 million years ago. The upper canines of saber-toothed tigers were extraordinarily long and in the shape of a dagger blade. They existed for several million years but then disappeared as they were unable to adapt to the changes in climate and vegetation that led to the extinction of their prey, the large herbivores, such as the mastodons.

The saber-toothed tigers' extinction does not mean that they were a poorly adapted or inferior species, simply that their teeth had become so specialized for a particular type of prey that, in evolutionary terms, the tigers became over-dependent on certain species.

The modern species of felines began to evolve at the end of the Miocene period roughly 10 million years ago, the most intense period for diversification of the mammals. This was the phase during which forests gave way to huge grasslands, allowing animals to collect and move in large herds. The current morphology of the felines has not changed much compared to that of their ancestors, but the appearance of those as large as a modern lion or tiger only occurred about 5 million years ago, which is a very recent period in terms of evolution. Fossils of cheetahs, leopards and lions have been found in Africa in stratifications dating to 3.2 million years ago.

By taking blood samples from wild and captive cheetahs, experts have shown that the individual animals share a very strong genetic identity. Thus skin transplants between animals that have no particular family link give rise to only slight reactions of rejection. Cheetahs seem to be as "related" as blood-related laboratory guinea pigs that have mated for generations! According to some scientists, the population of cheetahs suffered a series of drops in number during their evolutionary history, the first of which – about 10,000 years ago – was the most serious. The result was that they have since mated between "cousins," starting from a very restricted genetic group. The question of the sudden fall in the world population of cheetahs and its causes remain at the center of lively debate.

Another explanation for the lack of genetic diversity between cheetahs could be the huge number of "exchanges" that have taken place in a homogeneous environment between individuals that have progressively crossbred. In this system of reproduction, which specialists call the "Panmixia", individuals can mate with any other but it leads in time to genetic uniformity, as is the case, for example, with various types of weasel.

Of course, this is only hypothetical, but what are the consequences of this lack of genetic diversity among cheetahs? According to some researchers, it is responsible for the high rate of infant mortality, the low sperm count in males and a greater vulnerability to disease. Genetic variety is unquestionably important because a species is able to adapt on an evolutionary scale to changes in its environment; for instance, cheetahs are probably incapable of reacting to an epidemic in their population and are more vulnerable to certain types of virus. Cheetahs in captivity raise even greater worries. Their generally low reproduction rate is often linked to the conditions imposed by the zoo itself, as some can boast a high number of births. Peter Jackson, the president of the feline group at the World Conservation Union (UICN), claims that, with regard to semen, "though some males are sterile, others are incredibly fertile." Many males are able to reproduce in captivity and the success of mating attempts or reproduction are more likely to be linked to the conditions in which the animals live, such as the dimensions of the enclosures, the non-separation between males and females, and the choice of partner. Nothing seems to link the high mortality of cheetah cubs to their genetic homogeneity, and where experiments have been carried out on the reintroduction of the animals to areas where there are neither lions nor spotted hyenas, their population has increased considerably.

Felines and human beings have in common at least 60 hereditary sicknesses, certain carcinomas, diabetes and several pathologies of cardiac muscle. Biomedical researchers have therefore been very interested in felines, particularly so as the animals have long been in contact with viruses of the HIV family. This is especially the case with domestic cats, with a multitude of pets carried away by feline AIDS (FIV) due to destruction of their immune system.

32
This female cheetah, like her young son, climbs trees with extraordinary ease. For her, trees serve as ideal observation points.

33
A female leopard, safe and secure upon a trunk, observes some passing hyenas, not visible in the photo.

34

Lounging on a termite hill, a female leopard devotes herself to grooming, while her cubs rest on an acacia tree in the vicinity.

35

After a meal, a female cheetah cleans the pads and tops of her paws. An adult's claws do not retract completely; they are always visible.

The virus also strikes wild felines: the team led by researcher Dr. Stephen O'Brien (Chief, Laboratory of Genomic Diversity, National Cancer Institute, Washington, D.C.) has analyzed the DNA of wild members from 18 different species, and all were found to carry the FIV antibody.

In other words, they too had been exposed to the virus at some stage – the same is true of cheetahs, the lions in the Ngorongoro crater and the panthers (as leopards are termed) of Florida – yet they were all shown to be in good health.

How are wild felines able to escape the fatality that FIV condemns on domestic cats? It might be said that in nature the virus in some way seems to be "neutralized." Both cheetahs and leopards are vulnerable to scabies (a form of dermatitis caused by the demodex mite).

A great many mites live on the coat of most of the animals and a balance of health is retained as long as the host remains in good health, but when it begins to suffer physically, due to environmental factors, a lack of prey or an increase in predators like lions and hyenas, the organism's natural defenses are weakened, allowing the mites to multiply. These then create acute irritation and the host loses much of its coat. By continually scratching itself, the cat produces lesions that quickly become infected, and this secondary infection often causes the death of the creature. In addition to this problem, leopards may contract anthrax, rabies and a form of distemper.

Cheetahs and leopards are often confused in nature although their builds and the environments they inhabit are very different.

A cheetah has lovely "tear spots" that cover the face like make-up from the lower part of the eye to the lips, giving it a melancholy expression. The patterns of these spots are used by cubs to identify their parents. The creature's iris is a lovely orange and its eyesight amazingly good. It has few whiskers, which indicates that its life is mainly diurnal. A cheetah's coat varies in color from pale gold to ocher or a tawny brown, though among leopards even albinos and dark-colored individuals have been reported. In desert regions their coats are particularly pale.

Unlike the fur of other spotted felines, the cheetah's has many solid black spots except on the throat, which is white. Each creature has a particular pattern and, with a little experience, it is possible to recognize them by the spots on their faces.

The marks on the tail are formed by 4 to 6 dark rings toward the white tip. Their coat is thick on the shoulders and along the spine, with a sort of hairy "collar" on the shoulder blades. In southern Africa, particularly in Zimbabwe, some animals, known as "royal cheetahs," have a mutation in which black stripes run along their back. These are created by the transformation of little spots into large splashes of black, which are also seen across the rest of their gilded livery.

Africans have long believed that this creature was a cross between a leopard and the spotted hyena and was even classified as a species to itself. The misunderstanding was cleared up when a royal cheetah was born in a breeding center to parents with standard coats, so establishing that royal cheetahs were simply variations on the spotted leopard. A litter of cubs might contain both "normal" and royal cheetahs. The Sahara cheetah (smaller and less strong than its cousins in eastern and southern Africa) is distinguished by its much paler coat, white throat and stomach, and less evident black spots on its face and tail.

Apart from the cheetah's coat, the animal differs from other felines by its physique, which has evolved purely for high-speed running. The fastest animal on Earth, cheetahs can reach 68 mph over a distance of up to 450 yards. Its build is rather like that of a greyhound, with long, muscular but slender legs, a broad chest, an arched neck and a small head for minimal wind resistance. Combined with its light body, this build is ideal for sprinting. In the Serengeti, the average weight of an adult male is 95 pounds and 84 for a female, but cheetahs in southern Africa are larger, weighing up to 143 pounds. To achieve their extraordinary speed, cheetahs have had to pay an evolutionary price: their jaws are less powerful and their teeth are small, consequently, as we shall see, they are not able to fight predators like lions and hyenas, which steal their prey and eat their young. The smaller size of the roots of their upper canine teeth allows them to open their respiratory tract wider than any other feline, and this is because they have an enormous requirement for air when they are at full speed. Their breathing rhythm alters from 16 breaths per minute at rest to 150 while hunting. Despite its ideal build for running, cheetahs need to rest for almost half an hour after every demanding hunt.

Even their muscles have evolved to give them extraordinary acceleration: it takes them just 2 seconds to reach 47 mph from a standing start! But they have other physical features that contribute to their astounding sprinting capability, for example, the flexibility of their spine allows them to "fly" over the ground for almost 50 percent of the time they are running.

The spine arches upwards when the rear legs are stretched forward, so lengthening every stride considerably. Their claws are partially retractile, extending just enough to give them a good grip on the ground and achieve powerful acceleration. The animal balances on its claws, in the same way a sprinter balances on the spikes of his running shoes. This provides a great advantage, especially when zigzagging after a fleeing prey, but their claws wear down very quickly. Another feat of agility is the cheetah's ability to turn immediately in either direction regardless of which front leg its weight is resting on. Its long tail acts as a compensator and counterweight.

The leopard, which is more powerful than the cheetah, is a sublime fusion of strength and grace. Due to way it moves and its behavior, the leopard seems larger than it really is. Its weight is similar to that of an adult human, averaging 130 pounds but ranging from 82 to 200. The smaller female has an average weight of 110 pounds but has a range of 62 to 130.

Generally speaking, leopards that live in forests and wet regions are larger than those in dry regions.

The color of their coat varies according to the environment but also individually: they range from reddish-brown to ocher in the savanna, to yellowish-brown in the desert, dark and golden in the rain forest and darker still in high mountains. The creature's palest areas are the legs, throat and stomach. The variations in coat color have led some to describe more than 30 subspecies but today experts do not recognize more than 8, including the African leopard.

Its tawny coat with black eyespots allows the leopard to blend in more effectively with tall grass and leafy branches, passing almost unobserved. The back of the ears has a clear white mark on a black ground.

The melanic member of the family, known as the panther, or more specifically the black panther, is seen more commonly in rainforests and is more widespread in Asia than Africa. Its spots can be seen beneath the black fur.

A leopard's senses are very acute; it has the largest ears of the all the carnivores. Positioned somewhat forward, they give the animal a very precise idea of the distance from which a sound comes. Its pupils can open very wide, reaching their maximum dilation at night to allow as much light as possible to enter, but they are reduced to vertical slits during the day to prevent it from being dazzled.

The retina of felines differs from our own by the abundance of rods and scarcity of cones. The latter explain why cats have relatively poor color vision whilst the former are essential in conditions of little light. Whereas our eyesight is more acute, felines (particularly the cheetah) are better able to focus on the horizon, a valuable capability for a predator in open country.

In addition to an excellent sight and sense of smell, leopards have a wonderful sense of hearing, two or three times better than that of human beings and incredibly wide-ranging: they are able to hear any sound with a frequency of between 15 and 45,000 Hz (humankind's hearing ranges from 15 to 20,000 Hz).

When there is no light at all, leopards depend on their hearing, smell and the sensitivity of their whiskers to move. As a leopard moves, its whiskers brush against the surrounding vegetation, enabling the animal to judge the width of the space available to it. If the passage is too narrow, the leopard will avoid it, otherwise the rustle created by pushing against the vegetation would alert possible prey to its presence. When a leopard attacks, its whiskers bristle forward, which allows it to "feel" its victim and sink its teeth in the right place. It is also possible that a leopard's whiskers allow it to sense variations in the direction of the wind.

With their athletic physique, leopards can meet challenges gracefully. They can swim, cross a torrent, and climb the smoothest of tree trunks and steepest of rocks. In order to climb, they make use of very strong, retractable claws (five on the front paws and four on the rear ones). They are also powerful jumpers, and use their long tail to maintain their balance.

Their highly supple spinal column and short, muscular legs enable them to make long jumps. Curved like a bow, the backbone stretches out the moment the rear legs provide the thrust against the ground, thus creating propulsion like a spring. They can run agilely along branches without taking a wrong step, but it is above all their extraordinary suppleness and sinuous gait that gives them their

elegance. A leopard's tail reveals its mood: when it swings from side to side, the leopard is experiencing repressed tension. When it lashes the air or moves the tip up and down, it is a sign that the animal is preparing to charge. Its powerful jaws are equipped with 30 teeth: the sharp canines are to savage the prey, the incisors to grasp it and the molars to chew.

The leopard's tongue is lined with horny papillas and is almost a "rasp" made to lick its prey's bones clean.

Over its history, the leopard has undergone a gradual adaptation that has given it a series of perfect hunting weapons: teeth perfect for grasping and ripping flesh, a short, rounded skull, and muscular jaws so powerful that it can drag its victims with its fangs, lift them and carry them up into a tree. Even the muscles at the back of the neck have been developed for the same reasons.

At one time leopards lived across all of Africa except for the tropical forests and heart of the Sahara. In addition they inhabited vast regions of Arabia, Persia and India. Their progressive extinction first struck the Asian subspecies, then those of northern Africa and the Sudan.

Wild-life specialists assume that the cheetahs found in Iran are the last population of the Asian subspecies. The Saharan cheetah still lives in Niger, Mali and Algeria and perhaps south Libya. Roughly 50 individuals live in each of these countries. The destruction of their habitat and poaching have ensured that they no longer live in large numbers except for Kenya, Namibia, the Transvaal in South Africa, Botswana and northern Tanzania. In 1998 the world population of leopards totaled around 10,000 but in 1900 there were approximately 100,000.

Endangered to the west, the survival of this feline is more assured to the east and south.

Cheetahs need large, open and semi-arid spaces of thin, sparse grass with few bushes as it is unable to hunt effectively in tall grass and zones with dense arboreal vegetation. Naturally, it cannot reach its top speed if it is obliged to zigzag between obstacles. However, in South Africa, particularly Kruger Park and the regions neighboring Zimbabwe and Mozambique, the cheetahs inhabit an environment that is much more bush-clad than is normally congenial to the animal. They are also well adapted to life in arid environments, and they once used to live in the south of Algeria. Cheetahs do not have to find water frequently, for example, in the Kalahari Desert cheetahs can travel an average distance of 51 miles without drinking. They satisfy their physical requirement for liquids by drinking the blood and urine of their victims or by eating desert melons (*Cucumis colocynthis*). Currently, the distribution of cheetahs corresponds more or less precisely to that of gazelles, which also inhabit dry, open, desert or semidesert regions.

Leopards are perfectly adapted to a range of climates, both hot and cold. They inhabit forests, grasslands, mountains, plains, wetlands and deserts, and sometimes even agricultural estates.

In 1926 the frozen body of a leopard was even found in Kilimanjaro crater, at an altitude of 19,000 feet! But leopards live for the most part in wooded areas.

They are mostly active from dusk to dawn, leading secret and mysterious lives. They can also be seen by day in places where they feel completely safe. Adaptable and opportunistic, they are even able to coexist with man in urban districts. In 1978, the authorities calculated that some 50 leopards could be

found in Nairobi, where they lived on cats and dogs. Much more recently a mother and two cubs were spotted on a golf course in Karen, a suburb of the Kenyan capital. Leopards are also strong swimmers and have no fear of water.

In southern Africa, some leopards have survived on small islands following the construction of dams, at least as long as there was prey to be had. They then moved from island to island though this might mean swimming more than half a mile!

The cheetahs and leopards that we have closely observed over time live in the Masai-Mara Reserve in Kenya. Lying in the southwest of the country 160 miles from Nairobi, the Masai-Mara forms a unique ecosystem with the Serengeti National Park in Tanzania. Instituted in 1950, it was enlarged in 1961 to cover 556 square miles but only 240 of these are completely protected. In the other part, known as the ranch zone, the Masai herders raise cattle and live mostly in temporary villages. The Mara and its tributary the Talek are perennial rivers so that all year round there is marshland. There are also many seasonal and subsidiary water courses called *laga* in the plains. Bushes and trees grown on the banks of *laga* help create good climatic conditions that have made the Masai-Mara Reserve one of the richest wildlife zones in Kenya.

Relations between the species change constantly, both for herbivores and their main predators. Some populations are on the increase while others are in decline.

The rhythm of life in the reserve is marked by the migration of the gnu, which arrive from the Serengeti at the beginning of July and leave again toward October. Beginning in June, the whole reserve awaits the arrival of the hundreds of thousands of herbivores. Their migration is linked to the rains and so is never exactly predictable, either in terms of date or form.

We have been following the life of a family of leopards in "Leopard Gorge" for more than eight years. The gorge is filled with rocks, fig trees and euphorbia and has a special beauty that has remained unchanged. It provides a home to hyraxes, hyenas, vervet monkeys, agamid lizards and maybe a couple of porcupines.

We first saw Chui in 1991 and since returned to watch her at regular intervals. We saw her first female cub, Beauty, in 1993 when she was just a few weeks old. In November 1993 Chui gave birth to two more cubs, Mong'aa, a male, and Taratibu, a female, but Taratibu was killed at the age of two years by lionesses.

As for Mong'aa, he had many problems with the Masai in summer 1996: the herders wanted to kill him because he had got into the habit of eating their sheep. In February 1997 Chui risked death; the drivers of safari jeeps saw her with a Masai arrow stuck in her shoulder but she was set right when a vet from the Kenya Wildlife Service anesthetized and operated on her. A few weeks later she was able once more to play quite happily with her daughter Zawadi that was beginning to become self-sufficient.

In March 1999 Zawadi gave birth to her first daughter, but she died after just a few days. During summer 1999 Chui got caught in a trap while trying to enter a Masai village to take a goat or sheep – she was about 12 years old.

In October 1999 Zawadi had two more cubs.

The young male was killed by lionesses at four months, but Lisa, the female, survived. After the death of the male, Zawadi took Lisa far from Leopard Gorge to a rocky and inaccessible area, but now there

40
A male cheetah, endowed with a sharp sense of hearing, tenses as she listens to surrounding sounds.

41
Adult teeth appear in cheetahs only after about eight months. Having short canine teeth and a fairly weak jaw, this feline is unable to grind large bones.

42-43
The female cheetah and her cubs prefer areas of low grass, frequented by small Thomson's gazelles. In tall grass, however, they find other antelope species like nagors.

44-45
Male leopards are extremely strong, later in life they develop a dewlap of flesh that hangs from the throat and which can sometimes extend as far as the chest.

46 and 47
A female leopard has a drink after her meal. Leopards may drink every day, but are also able to abstain for several days at a time.

48 and 49
Leopards love forest zones where they can easily conceal themselves; they avoid open areas as much as possible. Cheetahs, on the contrary, have no use at all for trees.

is another female, Bella, who allows us to watch her cubs on the banks of the Talek.

These are the main animals in the population of leopards we will return to in this narrative.

Cheetahs have clearly increased in number in the northern section of the Masai-Mara Reserve in the 1980s and 90s, especially beyond its boundary in the ranch zone of the Masai. When traveling through this zone we were almost certain to see at least one adult cheetah every day, maybe more.

This was an area where many gazelles and impala browsed and there were fewer lions and hyenas than in the reserve itself. Owing to the Masai, these large predators only went out at night, leaving their daytime hiding places. By dark the cheetahs could quite happily hunt and move around with their cubs, so it was a perfect area for them.

More than 60 adult cheetahs lived in the Masai-Mara Reserve and its surrounds. Today the Masai have become more sedentary and take increasingly large herds into the ranch zone, grazing the grass too low, disturbing the cheetahs and destroying the hiding places needed to keep the cubs safe.

For two or three years it has been necessary to cross the river to find the cheetahs in the "Mara triangle" west of the water course. This is where various females regularly raise their cubs, in particular Douma, a cheetah we have been watching for a number of years, like her mother and grandmother before her.

Their territory lies on both banks of the river, and, when the water level is low, the cheetahs do not hesitate to cross in search of their favorite prey, Thomson's gazelle.

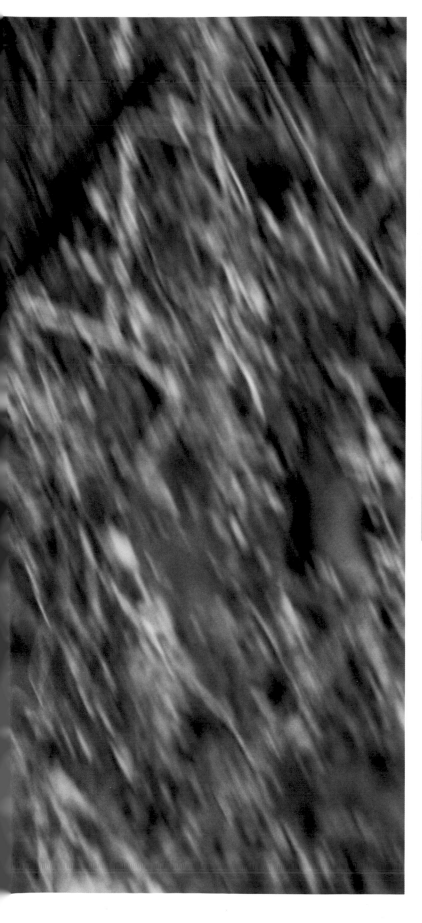

50 and 51
*A female leopard leaves to hunt in the late
afternoon, when the temperature drops, having
spent the whole day hidden among the dense
branches. Sometimes, in areas where they feel
undisturbed, leopards are also active during the
day, though they live above all by night.*

52 and 53
The leopard, being particularly agile and flexible and having strong claws, is able to climb up a vertical trunk. If the tree is not too tall or straight, leopards tend to descend them head first; otherwise, they climb down as they did up.

54 and 55
A mother cheetah and her cubs, respectively 16 and 2 months old, wait close to each other for the rain to subside, as do the nearby herbivores. As soon as the shower finishes, they shake off the water, then, in the sun, try to dry their fur.

56
*A leopard moves out in the open with a light,
sure step. The animal's rather wide paws give it
stability and, when necessary, speed.*

57
*Thin, long, and muscular limbs, a long and
narrow chest, and an arched neck: the cheetah
is slightly reminiscent of a greyhound.*

58 and 59
*This female leopard has just woken up, after
having spent the hottest hours of the day sleeping
under a bush. She stretches, then yawns,
revealing the sharp canine teeth that serve to
shred flesh.*

60

Female leopards without cubs spend most of the time sleeping and relaxing.

61

The leopard's sensory "whiskers" (vibrissae) are important; when the animal moves, they supplement visual information. For example, they provide an indication of the width of a passage, so that the leopard will not make noise by brushing against the sides.

62 and 63

The cheetah's spinal column is extraordinarily flexible. At a full run, it works like a spring that contracts and stretches. With each stride, the feline tries to lean far forward, making it possible for it to reach up to 47 miles per hour in two seconds.

*Although less agile than leopards in climbing up
and down trees, young cheetahs can nonetheless
perform elegant leaps.*

65

*A female leopard prepares to climb an acacia
tree, where she left her kill. It is amazing how
these felines can climb and sit on these trees
without getting any thorns in their paws.*

A mother cheetah takes advantage of her time with her young: she does not have to keep on alert, given that all of them are able to sense threats. Furthermore, predators avoid families with adolescents.

67
Every female cheetah lives on her own extensive territory, following the movements of her favorite prey.

68 and 69
The cheetahs of the Samburu Reserve, in northern Kenya, do not hesitate to wade through water to feed. It is shallow, so they "touch bottom."

70
A leopard stretches, working its extremely flexible spinal column: it allows the cat to perform acrobatic leaps when hunting.

71
A leopard's coat is very light on the belly and chest.

72
A male leopard marks his territory with urine.

73
After a long sleep on a termite hill, a female leopard stretches before leaving to hunt.

74
*Upon reawakening, a mother cheetah and her
cubs clean each other.*

75
*This six-month-old cheetah, after having played
vigorously with its brothers and sisters, begins
to yawn.*

SOCIAL RELATIONS AND SOLITUDE

76 left
A female leopard scans the terrain with her daughter.

76 right
After their afternoon nap, two adolescent cheetahs play quietly.

78
This female leopard cherishes certain spots within her domain, like the termite hill on which she is lounging.

79
It is not easy for a solitary cheetah to maintain its territory. Those unable to do so live a nomadic lifestyle.

The females of both cheetah and leopard species are solitary animals when they do not have cubs to raise.

Female leopards are territorial in their habits whereas female cheetahs lead more nomadic lives over a territory that is sometimes huge.

Each female leopard has her own territory which she uses for her daily activities and which provides her with the essentials of life: food, water, hiding places to bring up her cubs and the possibility of meeting males for mating purposes.

Each female uses only a part of her territory in a certain period depending on the presence of prey and the density of other predators, such as lions and hyenas. The territory may include inhospitable areas that are never used – for example, Zawadi (and Chui before her) spent a long period in Leopard Gorge, but was forced to leave as a result of the pressure exerted by the Masai.

The territories of different females may overlap either partially or completely, and it may be unavoidable that they meet even if they try not to. The meetings are generally peaceful, particularly as in many cases female leopards living on neighboring territories are from the same family, whether cousins, sisters or daughters. When a daughter leaves her mother, she generally occupies a territory nearby or even a section of her mother's.

The boundaries between territories are not rigidly defined and may alter depending on the size of the litter and the dominant relationships.

Violent clashes between females are rare and very few of them are scarred, however, a pregnant female or mother with young cubs will be aggressive. The risk of conflict is increased if the females that meet are not related.

Every female constantly marks her territory to signal to younger females or those migrating that the zone is occupied. This is why, when females become mothers, they soon leave their cubs alone in the den for the time necessary to mark their territory.

A female cheetah does not defend the territory she is occupying from other cheetahs, even if she marks it with her urine and excrement.

This is why the term "domain" will be used rather than "territory." If two females see one another whilst out and about, in most cases they will sit and stare at one another until one of them moves off. It might also occur that two mothers keep their cubs hidden a few hundred yards from one another but that they avoid direct contact.

Unlike what happens with other felines, the domains occupied by female cheetahs may be more than five times the size of those of the males. Once they become independent, young female cheetahs generally remain on the same domain as their mother. In the Serengeti a female's domain averages 500 square miles.

During the wet season most females occupy the plains where the grass is short. At the start of the dry season, if they are not hindered by the presence of very young cubs, they head northwest to the Seronera area where they remain from July to September. The reason for their shift is to follow the migratory movements of the Thomson's gazelles.

The distances they cover on such movements can be large.

Each female will use different areas of her domain depending on the time of the year, and will return to them annually. The domains of female cheetahs overlap to a considerable extent. At certain times of the year, many of them meet in areas where the concentration of prey is very high and hunting conditions favorable, for example, the short-grass plains where many gnu are born. This kind of zone is particularly attractive to the males.

Male leopards are solitary individuals of impressive size, on average double that of the females. A strip of skin hangs like a sort of beard from their thick necks.

A male leopard's territory is much larger than that of the females; it may be shared with several other males. For example, in the Kruger National Park, the territories of the males may cover between 6 and 36 square miles, roughly 6 times larger than the average territory of a female, which measures between 2 and 11 square miles. In certain areas of Africa, where prey are rare, the area needed for a leopard to survive may be as much as 160 square miles.

Sometimes the territories of males overlap at the edges or in less frequented areas. As the area to be protected is very large, a male cannot cover it all and in reality only defends its core, the section he uses the most.

Leopards in neighboring territories will certainly meet sooner or later, though they try to avoid such encounters, and are always aware of the other's strong and weak points. Males out reconnoitering have been observed advancing parallel to one another but each on his side of the territorial boundary. To intimidate his neighbors and any passing leopards, in addition to active defense, a resident male will mark his territory and use vocal communications.

He will always avoid a direct confrontation if possible as this brings risk. Conflicts generally occur following the intrusion of a new arrival or the death of a resident male, but an unoccupied territory will not remain empty for long as there are nearly always other males, the new generation for instance, ready to take it over.

Generally, resident males keep their hold over a territory for years. When a young male leaves his mother – a little like a lion – he remains nearby at first, gradually moving farther away before entering a nomadic phase of life. He moves far away from the territory he grew up in but often returns until he reaches maturity.

During his wandering, he tries to avoid the territories of other males or attempts to remain unnoticed, not marking the ground and remaining silent. In this way he minimizes the risk of sparking a hostile reaction on the part of the resident (which may be his father). If the occasion arises, he will eat the remains of the resident's kill.

80

Not all female cheetahs are good mothers: some never manage to raise their offspring to an adult age because, for example, they let predators get too close.

81

A female cheetah notices smells left by males whose territory she is passing through. She does not have a territory of her own, so she ranges an immense vital domain, following the movements of the prey.

Studies made in southern Africa have shown that large adult males for the most part tolerate the presence of young nomads and avoid injuring them, especially if the youngster demonstrates submissive behavior, such as lying on his side and exposing his throat. This tolerance will last provided the intruder does not lay claim to the territory or to a female but when the young male reaches the age of reproduction, and thus becomes a rival, the resident male will chase him away violently.

A sub-adult male has little chance of mating before winning his own territory, something that happens about three or four years of age. Leopards of both sexes are solitary creatures but years of observation have confirmed that they meet regularly without showing signs of hostility even when they have no desire to mate. On the other hand, cases also exist of females being killed by males.

Other males are happy to share their kills with their mothers, even when she has another litter of cubs to feed.

The social arrangements of male cheetahs are rather unusual: some live alone and others in "coalitions." In the Serengeti, 40 percent of male cheetahs are solitary, 40 percent live in a coalition with another male, and 20 percent with another two.

These coalitions are stable, permanent "societies" that may last an entire life time. Almost 80 percent of coalitions are formed by individuals from the same litter. Groups of three are often composed of two brothers and an unrelated male that joined the pair during his second or third year of life. Another factor also differentiates male cheetahs: some are territorial and other nomads, an aspect that has a

direct bearing on their lifestyles.

All males pay attention to smell and to the markings left on termite hills, rocks or tree trunks by other cheetahs, but these markings are only made by the territorial males, using urine or excrement. Nomadic cheetahs wander over enormous areas. Naturally the most territorial cheetahs are those that live in coalitions as it is easier to conquer a territory in a small group than alone, and much easier to hold on to it. Clashes that are often very violent occur between resident males and intruders to the territory. Many are injured or even killed during the fight. A slight wound may also lead to death from starvation as the cheetah may be made incapable of hunting successfully. This is the reason that the adult females in many populations of cheetahs often outnumber the adult males. A nomadic male that finds a territorial marking left by one or two cheetahs within the previous 24 hours quickly makes off in the opposite direction unless he is without hostile intentions.

In the Serengeti the male cheetahs' territories cover an average of 13.7 square miles, whereas nomads cover vast areas measuring up to 290 square miles though these areas largely overlap. The most sought after territories are those that include one of the famous "hot points" where females temporarily group during their seasonal movements. Males fight fiercely to conquer these territories because the possibilities of mating are very high. Naturally each male in a coalition has to share the females with his companions, but as the chances of mating are much higher for territorial groups, the advantages of group life are undeniable.

82
These adolescent cheetahs interrupt the long naps they take during the hottest hours of the day and indulge in some quiet play.

83
The leopard smells every odor left in its territory. The scent-bearing markings are produced by a substance, secreted by two glands located under the base of the tail, that mixes with the urine. Such "messages" last for a long time.

As nomadic males cover very wide areas, the possibility also exists for them to mate with a lone female in heat. Among the cat family, male lions also sometimes form associations so as to dominate over groups of females.

In the event of a fight with outside males, "allied" cheetahs cooperate perfectly regardless of whether they are blood-related or not.

Each member of a coalition remains with his companions voluntarily. They lick each other's coats clean and actively look for one another if they get separated. There is no dominant male, and they share their kills and females equally.

Scientists have noted another difference between males: resident males (and females too, it should be added) are generally in better health than nomads. This is probably the result of the greater anxiety nomads suffer and the great distances they have to cover.

They move more often after sunset and have been seen in the tall grass, where they seem to hide. They rarely rest on rocky outcrops where they may attract the attention of resident males. Barely half of the males that reach adolescence make it to adulthood.

When they become independent, young males wander off far from their mother, undoubtedly to avoid creating blood relationships. As large litters are no longer so common among cheetahs, many males reach the age of independence alone. Their chances of survival are therefore lower than those of the cheetahs fortunate enough to begin their phase of independence in family groups.

In order to reduce competition for food and territorial fights, leopards communicate through markings and vocal calls. Every day they sniff at bushes, rocks and tree trunks on their path to pick up the messages left by passing fellow-leopards. The chemical signals may last for several days, even weeks if the conditions are favorable. When a leopard wishes to mark a territory, he squirts a jet of urine infused with a strong scent secreted from his anal glands just below the base of the tail. He may also scratch markings on a tree or leave excrement. All these signals inform other leopards of the sex, age, sexual status and perhaps even identity of the animal that left them. These indirect forms of communication are very useful means of marking his environment and strongly reduce the chances of dangerous encounters taking place.

The vocal communications of leopards, although less dramatic than those of lions, are equally impressive. Territorial animals publicize their presence with their calls, and, when another leopard hears them, it may either ignore the call, take avoiding action or respond, creating a sort of duet. A female in heat will call frequently and repeatedly to attract the attention of males and will head directly toward a male that calls to her.

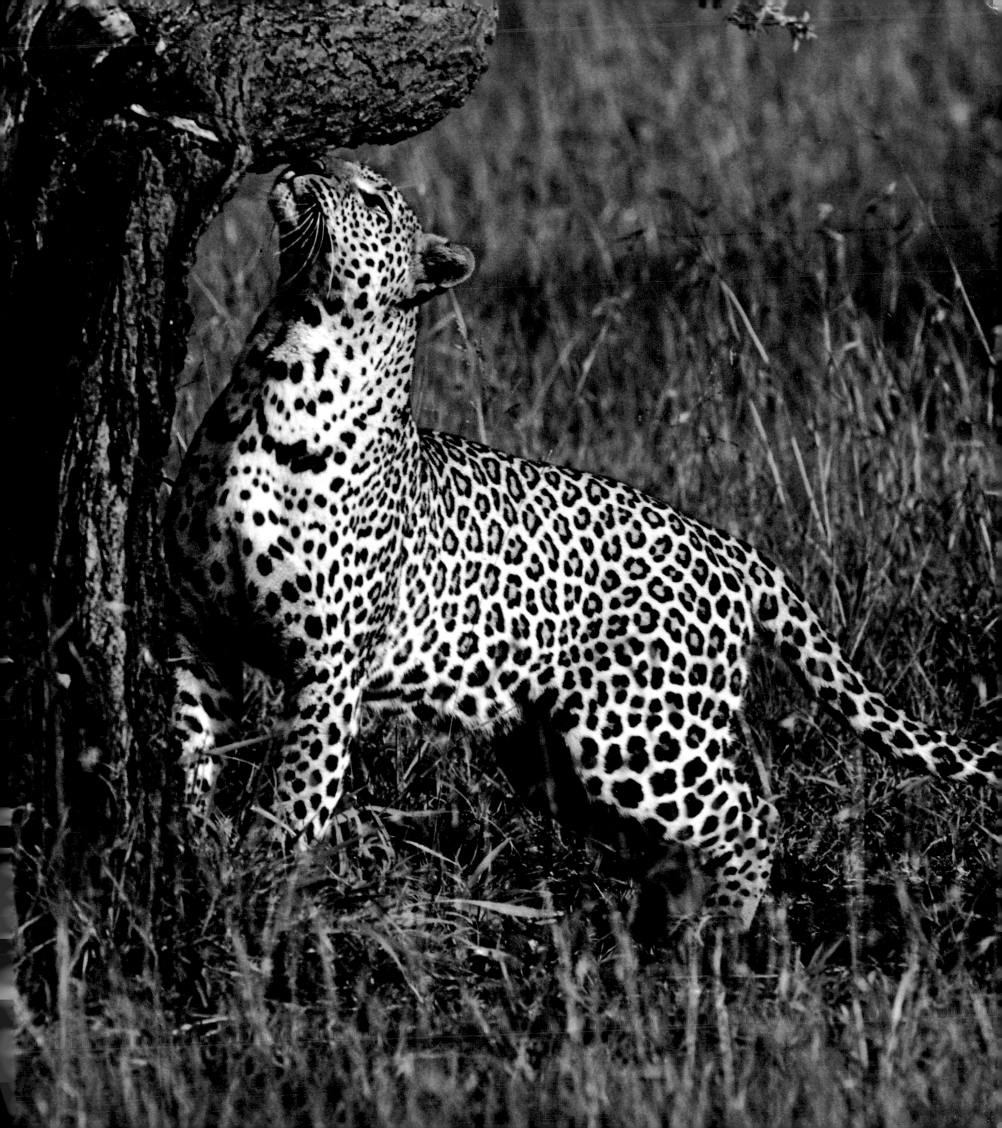

To show his presence in the territory, a male leopard mostly calls in the late afternoon when the animals restart their daily activities after the midday, or perhaps in the early morning before taking shelter. Leopards are rarely heard at night. Naturally, if a leopard is near a kill or, in the case of a mother, close to her cubs or den, the animal remains silent.

Resident leopards mostly make their calls when they are crossing zones of their territory where they may encounter a leopard from a neighboring territory. They generally keep a distance of 1000 to 3000 yards between them, which on average is the range of a leopard's call. When leopards find themselves face to face with creatures of the same species, or other predators, they snarl menacingly.

Hyenas take advantage of the calls of big cats to follow them and steal their food. Vocal communication is most often used during the dry season, when sounds travel best; markings are more effective during the rainy season.

Young males know more or less the position of territorial males from their calls and so take avoiding action. Young females do not make calls before the age of 24 to 30 months, the age at which they have matured enough to reproduce. Other calls are used by mothers to communicate with their offspring. They give out a low rumble when they return to their cubs after a hunt, and the cubs return a plaintive mew to claim their food.

These calls are low in volume as it is important not to attract the attention of lions, hyenas or other ancestral enemies, nonetheless, it gives them a varied language. Later, this same rumble is used by the mother and her grown cubs as a sort of friendly greeting and is used in a different way when she wishes to call them to order or make them follow her.

Cheetahs are very cautious. They usually sniff at piles of earth, termite mounds, tree stumps and all "strategic" points on their rounds. This allows them to recognize the identity of the territory's "owner" and to prevent them being surprised by a potential adversary.

Only territorial males mark such strategic points.

When they wish to remain in contact, mother and cubs emit a curious cry rather like the screech of a bird. They also use other sounds, all rather plaintive, short and strangely shrill for animals of their size. As the cubs grow, and with it their need to communicate over distances, the sounds are transformed into a sort of yelp that adults also use to communicate between themselves or by a mother to call her cubs to her when her normal cry has had no effect.

When they are happy, cheetahs purr, for example, when the mother greets or licks her cubs.

Like all felines, the ovulation of female cheetahs and leopards occurs by "induction." This means that the egg is only released from the ovary after mating has taken place.

Because the females of these two species live solitary lives, a female can never be sure that there

is a male around when she comes into heat, and thus the induction mechanism is particularly suitable.

If she is unable to couple, there is no ovulation and therefore she is very quickly once more "available."

A female leopard is receptive every 25–30 days. During her in-heat period (6–7 days), the hormonal composition of her urine and the nature of her anal glandular secretions altere.

It is highly probable that the male felines whose territories neighbor that of a female in heat will register her invitation because they often patrol their area and check the chemical messages left by females.

All felines have an organ in their palate referred to as Jacobson's organ, which has two openings behind the incisors. When the male smells the urine left by the female, he throws his head back, raises his upper lip in a kind of grimace and sucks in air. This allows him to assess the quantity of hormones in the urine.

To increase his chances of mating, a female in heat actively searches out males, leaving signals, making calls and covering great distances in her territory. Restless, she often stops to rub her head and muzzle against rocks or bushes or even rolls on the ground.

A male will mate with any female in heat he happens to find. A female may mate with the resident males close to her domain, but also with a nomadic male that succeeds in entering the patchwork of territories. This means that different litters may have different fathers.

Unlike lions, which mate in the open, leopards tend to couple away from possible observers, for example, in the depths of woodland or a dry riverbed.

It is the female that often takes the initiative, rubbing herself against the body of the male and then lying down on the ground. Like lions, the male bites the back of her neck and gives a loud grunt, to which the female will often react aggressively.

The coupling takes only a few seconds and is repeated several times. The male and female remain together for up to several days, sharing their kills.

A cheetah's periods in heat are short-lived but repeated at short intervals.

They reach sexual maturity very early, between 18 and 24 months. When a female in heat crosses a territory, she will couple with the resident male or males for several days, then goes off on her own, perhaps to join her young.

During the search for prey, a female may find herself – quite involuntarily – on the territory of one or more males. The "owners" may delay her for several hours or longer to see whether she is ready to mate.

It is possible therefore that a mother may be kept "prisoner" for various days, meaning that her cubs risk starving to death or falling prey to predators. Cheetahs' coupling is brief. If all goes well, the female may have a litter every 17 to 20 months. If the cubs die, she will mate again as quickly as possible.

86
By chance, a female leopard runs into her grown daughter, from whom she has separated for days.

86-87
This leopard's highly visible tail is an indicator to the antelopes that it is not hunting.

88
A female leopard sharpens her claws on a tree.

89
Though it stretches out completely to sharpen its claws on a tree trunk, this recently independent cheetah still does not know how to climb it.

90-91
After a rather peaceful coexistence, one fine day some young cheetahs, raised by two mothers not far from each other, fight ferociously. No one, however, will be hurt.

92 and 93
Young cheetahs, both male and female, chase and fight each other for fun. The fake battles are very useful and especially for the young males; as adults, they will have to fight for territory.

94 and 95
Grooming is a very elaborate process for cheetahs: it is an important means of socializing among felines.

96-97
Unlike the lions, cheetahs do not roar. They can, however, emit a range of sounds that vary from a high whimper to a sort of chirping noise.

HUNTING TO SURVIVE

98 left
A female cheetah strangles
a young impala.

98 right
In some regions of Africa, the
leopard has no rivals; he can
consume his prey on the ground
without being disturbed.

100
After a long chase, a leopard
rests, though it keeps an eye on
its surroundings and continues
to strangle its prey.

101
Her muscles tensed, a female
cheetah is ready to sprint.

An hour after sunrise, Douma, the cheetah we follow, wakes in the tall grass where she has spent the night. She stretches, cleans herself and sets off. She climbs a termite mound, marks it with her scent and gazes at the plain around her. Even with the vegetation so tall, she is able to understand what is going on.

We wonder what it is that directs her movements. We know where the herds of gazelle are but Douma seems to take the opposite direction. Suddenly a reedbuck jumps out a good way in front of the cheetah. These antelopes are solitary, hiding in the long grass or ditches near water. Douma sets off after the reedbuck but is unable to catch up in time, so abandons the chase. She slowly starts walking once again, still panting from the effort. For several hours she moves from one termite mound to another until she finally reaches the edge of the tall grass.

The plain before her caught fire a few weeks before but short green grass has already grown back. In the distance a dozen gazelles browse quietly. They are not aware of the cheetah, which remains perfectly still.

Douma begins to approach the gazelles slowly with her head stretched forward. One of the gazelles raises her head: Douma halts as though she were made of stone and waits until the antelopes start to graze again. Then she continues her approach, freezing every time one of the herbivores looks in her direction.

Douma's slow advance takes almost an hour. She seems to have her eye on a fawn of about a month old that is grazing next to its mother.

Once she is about 100 yards from her target, Douma shoots off at an incredible speed. Cries of alarm are given off and the gazelles flee in all directions.

The fawn has a last dart and bound as Douma catches up, but she knocks it off balance with a strike of her paw and then sinks her teeth into the gazelle's throat to suffocate it. Panting, Douma tries to catch her breath as she looks around worriedly.

She needs about a quarter of an hour before she will be able to eat. When she does, it is hurriedly and always on the alert. The sun is getting lower and lions can be heard roaring not far away. Three hyenas arrive from the opposite direction and Douma hurries off, leaving them the rest of her meal. After putting some distance between herself and the hyenas, she stops for the night in a rocky area.

The next morning Douma does not seem to intend to hunt, but nonetheless she succeeds in surprising a hare in the undergrowth. She passes the rest of the day asleep. The following morning we find her in an area of short grass where she has been seen by the antelopes. With their eyes on the cheetah, they follow her movements as she advances from a safe distance. Douma knows she has no chance of making a kill in these conditions so she decides to change hunting ground. From the top of a hill she spies a herd of impala and, very unusually, she advances on them completely in the open.

The impala flee, followed by Douma though not at her top speed. She is trying to find a weaker animal that is not as fast as the others, but she is not satisfied by the result and goes to lie down in an area where the brush is thicker while she waits for the impala to forget her.

After a couple of hours the antelopes show no sign of worry, and some Grant's gazelles are also approaching, unaware of the danger. One of the males begins to graze close by and Douma, with all her senses at the alert, prepares to attack. We watch, caught up in the tension of the moment. The attack is short-lived. Her prey tries to zigzag in front of her but the surprise of the attack was too great and in less than 200 yards Douma has brought the gazelle down.

Knowing that Douma sleeps the whole day after such a large meal, we leave to search for our leopard Zawadi, which we had seen at dawn close to the large fig tree she seems to like. Our attention is suddenly caught by the almost intact carcass of an impala on the forks of a large tree. Thinking that it was Zawadi's kill, we wait for her.

The ability of leopards to carry their victims into a tree where they can return to feed on them often helps us to locate them. All that is needed is patience, and to wait for their return when they are not too ferocious.

The day passes. Vervet monkeys play among the bushes close by. Suddenly their cries of alarm put us on our guard: Zawadi is walking up the dry riverbed behind the tree. If it had not been for the monkeys, we would not have known she was there. She is almost invisible. With a bound she reaches the fork where she left her kill. Taking it in her jaws, she carries it back down the trunk, thenclimbs an acacia not far off but which is less easily seen from our vehicle. Staying a certain distance away, we watch her eat for almost an hour.

Then, she licks her fur, climbs down to drink from a pool and relieve herself, thenclimbs back up the tree where she spends the night. We hear hyenas calling but Zawadi ignores them; she knows that in the tree she is safe from her most fearsome rivals. The next morning she takes another meal from the carcass and returns to the tree that evening. During the night, she disappears among the bushes. We look for her over the next few days but in vain.

Then, one morning, we see her at dawn as she walks slowly between the rocks in a ravine. Around nine o'clock she stops and lies down to let the dew on her coat dry in the sunshine. Not far away some hyraxes have come out in the open and are only separated from the leopard by a few bushes. Zawadi has seen them and begins to creep closer. She freezes, staring at her victim just a few dozen yards away.

She advances yard by yard, just as her mother Chui had done in the same place a few years before. When the hyraxes see her, it is too late. She launches herself at one of them and pins it down with her claws. Little more than a snack, the hyrax is swallowed in just a few mouthfuls. The favorite prey of cheetahs in East Africa is the Thomson's gazelle. This species represents about 60 percent of all their kills in the Serengeti and about 42 percent in the Masai Mara Reserve; in the latter, impala represent another 30 percent or so of their diet.

102
Staying low to hide her light-colored belly, a female leopard approaches her prey.

103
The young female leopard Beauty leaps on a francolin. Still inexpert (she is a year old), she hunts mostly small prey.

In the semi-arid biotope of northern Kenya, the small kudu, dik-dik and gerenuk are their most common prey. In southern Africa cheetahs like equally springboks and puku, the latter being herbivores about the same size as Thomson's gazelles. In the Sahara, cheetahs feed principally on Dorca gazelles, rodents, foxes and birds. During the breeding season, cheetahs mostly catch gazelle fawns but also the young of large species, such as topis, greater kudus and gnus, but they do not disdain small prey like hares (especially in the Serengeti) or guinea fowl or francolins.

Sometimes they will even attack adult warthogs but these can be very dangerous, much more so than a gnu protecting her young even though all the big cats – especially lions and leopards – eat a large quantity of young warthogs. A female warthog will not hesitate to charge a cheetah or leopard if her young are threatened, forcing the predator to abandon its victim and flee to avoid being injured.

When their natural prey is lacking, cheetahs will even attack cattle, and farmers in Namibia consider cheetahs a harmful species. In the Masai-Mara, however, they rarely attack the herds belonging to the Masai.

Considering the size of its victims, experts have calculated that cheetahs catch on average between 150 and 300 animals a year in the Serengeti, as opposed to the 29–30 caught by lions. Unlike lions, cheetahs never return to finish the remains of their kill and do not feed on carcasses, which protects them from being poisoned by rotten meat. Male cheetahs that hunt in a coalition are able to add to their menu adult or sub-adult gnus, as well as other large antelopes, something solitary females are unable to do.

Leopards attack a large variety of animals. Their diet ranges from termites to a broad assortment of antelopes that may weigh individually up to 440 pounds. Then there are such creatures as freshwater crabs, frogs, mongooses, termites, beetles, various types of birds, lizards, hares, hyraxes, monkeys and baboons. Studies carried out in Londolozi in southern Africa have shown that leopards' prey is largely composed of three species: impalas, duikers and warthogs.

Some leopards in the Masai-Mara Reserve regularly attack white storks migrating to and from Europe and carefully pluck out their feathers before eating them. Others eat fish after catching them with their paws in shallow water. Others are prepared to feed on porcupines, anteaters and snakes.

Hearing the cries of a duiker in the coils of a python, a leopard was once seen watching the snake as it swallowed its victim, then to attack it, and strike it on the head so that it was obliged to give up the duiker to the leopard, which then made off with it! Another leopard, this time in the Aberdare Mountains in Kenya, succeeded in driving out dung beetles by delving its paw into a pile of buffalo dung. They will even eat predators like civets, genets and jackals.

A sample of 150 kills made by a leopard in the Serengeti revealed 30 different species, whereas the same number of kills in a lion's diet counted just 12.

The high number of species on which leopards feed indicates that as predators they are opportunists, much more so than either the cheetah or lion. Indeed, there are few animals a leopard could not kill

when prompted by hunger. And more than other large African cats, it attacks domestic livestock like sheep, goats, calves, and sometimes adult cattle or dogs.

Most of the prey leopards catch weighs less than 110 pounds even though they are able to kill animals that exceed their own weight. Once Zawadi's mother, who weighed barely 90 pounds, killed a buffalo of almost 275 lbs. A male leopard in the Mara reserve attacked an injured male gnu weighing 500 lbs and managed to suffocate it after a very long struggle. In addition to being opportunists, every leopard has its own tastes.

Certain leopards even have their particular preferences and will always hunt the same type of prey, ignoring others that may be easier to catch at certain times of the year.

Along with tigers and lions, leopards are also known as man-eaters. Such an event generally only takes place in exceptional circumstances, for example, when destruction of its native habitat obliges them to leave the depths of the forest or savanna and encroach on villages. The phenomenon is rare in Africa but more common in Asia. Africans that share territory with leopards fear attacks on livestock rather than their own persons.

Like lions, leopards can feed on carcasses if necessary. They will not hesitate to eat the victims of other predators and it is possible to attract them by leaving carcasses out, as some African tourist lodges do. For the same reason, they can be easily poisoned.

In nature, two types of hunting dominate: the ambush and the chase. Predators that follow their prey, like hyenas and African wild dogs, have developed speed and stamina. The cats tend to ambush their victims by making use of their "camouflage coats," which allow them to hide unseen; consequently, they do not have great stamina. A cheetah, for instance, will give up on the chase after just 300 yards of sprinting and the leopard after just 50 yards if the surprise attack does not produce the desired effect.

Both cheetahs and leopards prefer to attack young, old, sick or wounded animals than adults in possession of all their means of defense. When these cats tackle large prey with sharp horns, they have to bring the creature down with the minimum risk of being gored. Once they catch up with their victim, they tip it over with one or both front paws, making it fall to the ground. They then grasp its throat in their jaws and suffocate the animal. If the prey is small, they kill it by snapping the backbone at the level of the neck, causing immediate death.

Apart from these points in common, the techniques the cheetah and leopard use vary in relation to their individual builds and differing habitats.

Two main aspects differentiate the cheetah's hunting technique from that of the leopard: it hunts in the open plain and exclusively during daylight hours, preferably between 7 and 10 a.m. or from 4 to 7 p.m. By doing so it is less in competition with the lion and leopard, which mostly hunt by night. Has the cheetah's preference for daytime hunting always existed or was it the result of pressure exerted by the other large carnivores? This is a very difficult question to answer. It is exceptional for a cheetah to hunt by night, though it may occur at full moon.

It is difficult to describe a cheetah's typical day, which will vary depending on whether the animal is solitary or, in the case of a female, has cubs to feed. If a solitary cheetah makes a large kill, it may spend the next two or three days without hunting again. However, as soon as a cheetah feels hungry, it sets out shortly after dawn to track down a meal. It will stretch out and scrutinize the horizon, but if it does not see anything of note, it will climb to a higher point – like a termite mound or tree trunk – from where it can see farther. It patrols its domain, passing from one observation point to another, until it sees prey or until the heat is too great. At a certain point it has to decide which is greater, its desire to stretch out in the shade or its hunger. Cheetahs do not choose the shade of a tree or bush at random, as they prefer to have an open view, at least in one direction. Then they will give in to a light doze, though ready to start up if a gazelle should approach.

The only large predator able to run faster than its prey, cheetahs advance slowly in the direction of a herd of antelope, without attempting to hide. When the antelopes run away, the cheetah chooses its victim from the herd. Alternatively, it will advance without letting itself be seen, halting when the antelopes stop grazing. This second type of advance may last a long time. Once the victim has been chosen, the cheetah does not change its mind. It only sets off on the attack after having got close enough to its target. Although a cheetah can reach a speed of 68 mph, most measurements have shown speeds less than 56 mph. The animal must not fling itself too quickly into a sprint or the intended victim will manage to escape as it has more stamina. After 450 yards at breakneck speed the cheetah has to stop to catch its breath. Experiments have shown that during a sprint its temperature can rise to 104°F! If it continues to make such an effort, the cheetah will sustain brain damage.

Despite its physical capabilities, the cheetah, like other felines, is a sprinter and not a long-distance runner. Unlike gazelles, its evolution has not given it the capacity to stand high temperatures. The gazelle cools itself by panting, and this allows it to inhabit very arid environments where the temperatures are high. A Thomson's gazelle will start panting when its body temperature reaches 109°F, and a Grant's gazelle can even withstand 114°F before it begins to cool itself down, but, like other species, the temperature of its brain must not exceed 105°F or it will suffer.

Consequently, gazelles always keep their brain temperature cooler than their body temperature by means of an interesting physiological adaptation. Their blood reaches their brain via the external carotids, which divide into hundreds of arterioles at the base of the skull and cross over a veined sinus. The blood passing through the arterioles is cooled by between 37 and 42°F in the nasal mucous through water evaporation. Thus the more the gazelle pants, the cooler its blood becomes.

When a cheetah has chosen a young gazelle as its victim, it can begin its run at the herd from farther away because it will be able to reach the gazelle without having to exert itself overly. Cheetahs can easily follow a zigzagging animal because their claws give them a strong grip on the ground and their long tail, which acts as a counterbalance, provides them with greater stability during the changes of direction.

106
Cheetahs, like leopards and lions, prefer to attack very young animals, or elderly, sick, or wounded ones, rather than adults in their prime. They are nonetheless good hunters, very careful in tracking prey and in not launching their attack before they are sure of themselves.

107
Surveying the surroundings, these 10-month-old cheetahs help their mother (seen from the back in the foreground, her jaws gasping a gazelle by the head), who in turn can kill the prey undisturbed.

If the attempt fails, they require almost half an hour of rest before being able to try again.

Cheetahs are considered good hunters and on average half of their attempts end in success. In the Serengeti plains the success rate varies between 37 and 69 percent when hunting adult Thomson's gazelles but is 100 percent with their fawns. This rate is much higher than that of the lion, which achieve rates of 15–30 percent, and the leopard, which achieves a 5–10 percent rate. Perhaps cheetahs, which burn so much energy in their sprints, have learned to assess their probability of success better than their rivals. When they reach their victim, they trip it up with a paw. They usually use the claw of the thumb on their front paw, which is particularly sharp as it never touches the ground.

Studies by Dr Sarah Durant, a scientist with the Zoological Society of London, in the Serengeti have shown that solitary cheetahs (females and some of the males) prefer areas where there is a lower concentration of prey and competing predators. As we have seen in person, cheetahs face more difficulties when there are large numbers of gazelles in the plains as the many "sentinels" will give the alarm. A solitary cheetah will generally choose isolated Thomson's gazelles or those in small groups in the tall grass as they are less vigilant. According to Durant, such gazelles are usually males, and analysis of the kills clearly shows that males are the most frequent victims.

Male leopards that live in a coalition hunt larger animals than Thomson's gazelles, such as buffalo, gnu or warthogs. The larger the coalition, the larger the prey they will hunt. Thus, it is possible that a group of male leopards will pass through a herd of Thomson's gazelles in the direction of gnu spied a mile or more away without even attempting to bring down a small antelope. But even solitary males, when they are vigorous and strong, can bring down large herbivores.

This is the case with an old male called Mzee that lives in the Masai-Mara Reserve and which regularly attacks adult gnus. Tim Caro (a wildlife biologist at the University of California at Davis who has studied predators in Serengeti National Park) has made a detailed study of the hunts undertaken by groups of adult males or by young males that have just left their mothers.

As with other predators that live in a group, it is difficult to show that the fact of hunting together significantly increases the chances of success. Members of a coalition show little coordination during a hunt; in fact, certain individuals do not hunt at all, but just follow so that they are on the spot when the kill is made.

Caro's study shows that males in a coalition hunt together and at the same time in 66 percent of cases, that they attack the victim simultaneously 40 percent of the time, but rarely attempt to bring the victim down together. However, the fact of acting in a group reduces the risk run by individual hunters of not being able to defend their kill against other predators, even their own species, and therefore of each succeeding in winning a greater quantity of meat.

When adult gnus defend their young, one of the members of the coalition will occupy the adult while the others attack the victim.

Studies have shown that coalitions do not really

have more success at hunting than solitary animals, nor do they hunt more often.

From the point of view of food, the main advantages given by group hunting is that the members are able to attack larger prey and that they can eat their fill more than solitary animals, particularly during the dry season when it is more difficult to find nourishment. Occasionally males will steal kills from the females, but this occurrence is rare.

Leopards mainly hunt at night thanks to their penetrating nighttime vision, though they also hunt by day if the heat is not excessive. Analysis undertaken in southern Africa of a number of hunts shows that leopards generally set out at nightfall and search for prey until about 10 p.m. They then rest for two or three hours before restarting. If the second attempt also produces nothing, they rest once more and try again just before dawn. This third attempt may last while it is still cool. If a female has cubs, she will return to suckle them during the resting periods.

An expert at camouflage, a leopard tracks its prey in silence, almost invisible to man. It is possible to pass just a few yards from a leopard without being aware of its presence. The soft pads on its toes and sole, and the fine, soft hairs on the inside of the legs, perfectly muffle the noise produced by its movements. When walking normally, the pale areas on its belly and legs and the upright tail are visible to herbivores, but when a leopard is hunting it moves close to the ground, very tense, almost like a reptile, without taking its gaze off its prey. A leopard's highly sensitive whiskers and eyebrows allow it to judge the breadth of a narrow passageway. It does not always

advance at a steady pace but stops often to smell the scents in the environment and listen to the noises. Sometimes it raises its face above the height of the grass to see better. It might also sit for a moment, lie in wait next to paths used by different species of mammals, or rest on a large termite mound covered with vegetation for a better view. Once a victim has been singled out, the leopard will approach with extreme patience. The moment the prey shows the slightest disquiet, the leopard freezes. Studies made in Kruger National Park in South Africa suggest that, unlike a lion, a leopard is aware of the changes of direction of the wind during its advance, and that, should the wind change, it will take avoiding action so that its prey will not smell its presence.

The success of a hunt is based on the leopard's ability to anticipate the movements of its prey. The predator silently moves as close as it can without being seen, then it launches itself forward to take its prey by surprise. Leopards can get much closer to their victims than either cheetahs or lions. But despite their aptitude for hiding in the undergrowth, it is not always so easy. For example, a herd of gazelles or impalas is like a large number of eyes, noses and ears, all of which are perfectly designed to perceive the approach of a predator. The feline will stare at the herd, examining its movements, and try to position itself so that the herbivores will move toward it. Ideally, the prey will advance toward the predator, which lies perfectly still in the grass. If the herd changes direction, the leopard has to review its strategy and prepare its ambush a little way off.

When the distance between the leopard and victim is less than 10 yards, the leopard unleashes its attack

108
Newly adult cheetahs – and therefore independent, after being abandoned by their mother – have managed to catch a hare. It is not much of a meal for them, but their parent no longer brings down prey for them, and they still have difficulty in hunting antelopes.

109
As the sun sets on the horizon, a female leopard awakens after a long sleep atop a termite hill.

with a spring of the hind legs. It is only at the last moment that the victim becomes aware of the danger. The leopard falls upon it at a speed of 37 mph and rolls the prey over beneath its own weight, even if the predator is much lighter than the prey. A leopard may go straight for the victim's throat; in fact, the feline's body has evolved for this moment of the attack: it is able to leap up to 20 feet in a single bound, and its powerful jaws allow it to kill mammals three times heavier than itself in just a few minutes.

Rather than searching actively for prey, another possibility open to leopards is to remain hidden among the bushes, in a dry riverbed or between the branches of a tree. It may remain there for hours, hidden by the undergrowth or leaves, until a chance presents itself. Some leopards attack their victims from above but this is not seen everywhere. Studies made in Londolozi Game Reserve on leopards' hunting techniques have shown that they do not jump down on their prey from trees, perhaps because the undergrowth is very thick.

Some hunting techniques are very surprising, for example, a female leopard that had failed to catch an impala later went to lie down on a termite mound where she knew there was a warthog den. She waited there for more than an hour until the mother arrived with her young. She had chosen a position so that the warthog was dazzled by the sun and the wind carried her smell in the opposite direction, therefore not warning the warthog. This is not an exceptional case. It is not uncommon for a leopard to catch warthogs as they return to their lair, and if a leopard smells one that has already entered, it may wait above the opening until it comes out. Certain young

leopards even manage to enter the warthogs' lair and come back out with a baby, but this is a very hazardous move as warthog mothers can be very dangerous!

Leopards always economize their movements to avoid wasting energy. Their build and physical capacities do not allow them to hunt in the bare, open grasslands like the cheetah. If they do not succeed in catching their prey almost immediately, they do not give chase because they know they cannot keep up. Predators in wooded areas, leopards walk as quietly as possible, not just to approach their prey but also to avoid being seen by their strongest rivals: lions and hyenas. When a leopard has been seen by its potential prey and guinea fowl, monkeys and antelopes have given cries of alarm, it prefers to make off quickly if it is in an area where there is a concentration of large predators. Alternatively, it continues to move normally but with its tail erect and visible, thus signaling to the herbivores that it knows that it is not worth the effort to try.

A leopard will use hearing, vision and smell to identify its prey, with hearing perhaps being the most important sense. Leopards react to a large variety of sounds, which range from an antelope's alarm cries to a slight rustle in the grass – even if the prey is still invisible. They may even find their future victims from the scents they leave, and follow the trail, perhaps over long distances.

The leopard's success rate in hunting is very low, but this fact may not be very significant as it can repeat its attempts. Each time it uses up little energy, especially when compared to the effort expended by a cheetah. When the number of potential victims is

110
*Six-month-old cheetahs enjoying
a drink.*

111
*A female cheetah suffocates a
gazelle: it is a matter of minutes.*

112-113
*An attentive leopard watches gnus
migrating through the Masai-Mara.*

114
*A female leopard has killed an
impala in the Samburu Reserve.*

114-115
*Clutching by its throat, a leopard
carries the impala it has caught.*

116-117
*Often the leopard, like the lion,
feeds on carrion and eats prey
killed by other animals.*

high, as happens when the migrating gnu arrive with their young ones, leopards (and lions) may store up food for later.

Once at dawn we saw four or five carcasses of young gnus hauled up in the branches of trees a short distance from one another. The leopard returned to eat them all, for some of them over a period of days. It had perfectly memorized its storage places. It had not killed for pleasure, but simply taken advantage of a good opportunity, even if its stomach was already full.

After the exertion of the chase, a cheetah is exhausted. Panting, it has to rest for about 20 minutes to recover its strength, all the while watching out to ensure it is not surprised by other predators that have picked up on the clues left by the chase: cries and the scattering of the herd or the dust thrown up by the sprinting cheetah.

Compared to its rivals, the cheetah is at a disadvantage because it is unable to defend its trophy by force. It is not equipped to do so and is unable to carry its prey into a tree, like a leopard, where it would be protected. Consequently, in order not to be injured, often it is obliged to give up its prey to a larger animal, such as a lion, hyena, leopard or even a male baboon. It might be said that a cheetah only survives by giving up its meal to others, and this facet of their behavior has become so ingrained that even jackals or vultures can chase a cheetah away from its kill without difficulty.

As soon as it has rested, a cheetah can begin eating. Always on the alert, it rapidly tears away pieces of meat and bolts down small mouthfuls. It usually begins with the meat on the back as it is rich in protein, though other felines often prefer the internal organs.

If it is disturbed, the cheetah will abandon its kill and not return. Unlike lions, cheetahs do not eat kills made by other animals. An adult cheetah needs roughly 6.5 pounds of meat a day but might devour 30 in a single meal, then not eat again for several days.

After making a kill, a leopard will drag or carry its victim by the throat like lions. It can climb up a tree carrying an animal weighing 220 pounds in its jaws. Once it has done that, it no longer has any need to rush its meal; safe from hyenas and lions, it is also hidden from vultures. In the Masai-Mara Reserve, where there are many rival predators, leopards almost always take their kills into the trees. In Tsavo National Park they do so a little less often, and in some parts of Africa not at all. This means simply that they have no fear of being attacked. When faced by lions, a leopard – which is solitary and much less strong – has to surrender its catch, likewise with hyenas as they hunt in a pack.

When a leopard has a carcass hidden in a tree, its behavior is regular. It will return several times to eat, also spending time resting in the tree or on the ground or seeing to its physical needs. Every so often it will go off to drink.

118 and 119
Leopards survive even when the antelopes grow rare. Hares,
small monkeys, rock rabbits, guinea fowl, and even frogs and
fish can sustain them. Some leopards in the Masai-Mara will
venture as far as the manyattas of the Masai to attack their
livestock, sometimes getting themselves killed.

120 and 121
In the Masai-Mara, where hyenas and lions are
very numerous, the leopard always carries its
prey up a tree. Then, once it has safely stashed
its victim, it no longer needs to hurry to eat.

122
A leopard that has carried a big carcass up into a tree will return several times to feed on it its high, safe refuge. This practice or returning helps naturalists to encounter this very shy animal more easily.

123
A leopard often moves its kill from one tree to another as it seeks a more shady and comfortable spot.

124 and 125
*The cheetah has an almost 100 percent success
rate when hunting recently born gazelles: the
easy prey poses no risks. The cheetah, the
fastest animal on earth, can hit 68 miles per
hour. Furthermore, its spinal column's flexibility
enables it to "fly"; it does not touch the ground
for 50 percent of its total running time.
Nonetheless, despite its abilities as a sprinter,
this cat never chases its prey for more than a
half-mile because it requires enormous energy to
maintain sufficient speed.*

126 and 127
A cheetah chases a gazelle which attempts to escape by running in a zigzag. However, it is to no avail. Because its claws never fully retract, the cheetah can count on good ground traction at all times; it can abruptly change direction even at top speed, using its two- to three-foot tail for balance. Then, once it has clutched its prey in its front paws, the cat makes the gazelle lose balance and pins it to the ground.

128 and 129
Unlike lions and leopards, cheetahs only eat prey
caught by themselves or, if young, by their mother.

130
Although her cubs unable to follow her on the
hunt, the female cheetah will call them to join
her if she has killed nearby. If her kill is far
away, she will return, often after hours, carrying
the prey in her jaws.

130-131
Male cheetahs hunting in a pack are able to kill
large antelopes as adult or sub-adult gnus,
something solitary females can never do.

132-133
A mother cheetah always lets her cubs eat first.
When the kill is meager, she will have to hunt
again to feed herself.

SPECIES AGAINST SPECIES

134
A horde of vultures, having spotted the cheetah's kill from above, have landed around the feline.

136
The cheetah decides to chase off the nearest intruders, but soon it will have to clear the field once the competition becomes too numerous.

137
No sooner has a female cheetah killed an antelope when a hyena races over and snatches it away. The cat observes the "thief," letting it go without reaction.

The gazelles have melted away and Douma and her cubs are forced to change hunting ground. After searching for her for several days, we find her near the Tanzanian border. The packs of hyenas have increased greatly in this area since poachers have been coming in and killing animals for meat.

"The Daltons," as we call the fun-loving cub now 4 or 5 months old, are playing on acacia trees. While we arrange our vehicle to be able to watch them better, Douma loses no time: she is already suffocating an impala. The youngsters come down from the tree and approach their mother, but a hyena comes up and steals their kill. About 8 o'clock the next day, Douma kills a gazelle. The Daltons begin to eat straightaway but, as on the day before, the hyenas arrive. Terrified, the cubs bound in all directions. Douma faces up to a hyena for a few seconds but does not fight as the risk is too great.

The hyenas make off with the gazelle. Douma has to hunt once more, which she does about midday when the temperature is about 95°F in the shade. This the time of day when the antelopes look for shelter from the sun and the lions and hyenas rest. The days pass.

The female cheetah learns to deal with the problem posed by the hyenas to perfection. She avoids hunting early in the morning, preferring to wait until the hyenas rest in the heat of the day. In this area it is the only way for her to hold onto her prey.

Nonetheless, Douma gets robbed of another impala when a hyena arrives before she has even finished suffocating her prey. But the hyena meets the same fate at the hands of a male lion! Honey has had a similar problem: she has been robbed of her kill by two male baboons. It is not easy for a cheetah to hang onto its property!

Chui, the female leopard, advances cautiously along the ravine, her head low, stopping every so often to sniff for the presence of other predators. Suddenly she stops short, at the alert with her ears pricked.

One of the smells left by a lioness is particularly fresh. It is different to that of a cheetah or another leopard. Chui hesitates. Her experience has taught her that lions are dangerous, and that she would have little chance of survival in a fight with an animal that weighs three times as much as she does. Furthermore, Chui has already had one nasty experience, when she was forced to spend a few hours trapped on the highest branches of an acacia while the group of resident lions circled the trunk. Although they can climb certain trees, the lionesses that time were unable to compete with the leopard's agility.

After a siege lasting several hours, the lionesses went off, perhaps driven by hunger.

In theory, cheetahs and leopards are not direct competitors as they have different preferences in terms of environment and prey, but any interaction between the two species works in favor of the leopard. In exceptional circumstances, a leopard may kill a cheetah and drag it up a tree, in the same way that it would with the carcass of an impala. Lions kill and eat leopards and cheetahs but it is the cubs that are particularly at risk from other species. Cheetahs are not very aggressive creatures; in fact, their name in the Tuareg language – *tamachek* – means "fearful one." This is especially evident in the behavior of the mothers, who rarely defend their cubs from attack as they do not have the capability to do so. The cubs are therefore very vulnerable and suffer at the hands of other carnivores like hyenas, leopards and lions. If one of these predators threatens her cubs, a female cheetah has few possibilities of action. She might try to attract the attention of the predators by snarling and blowing, stamping on the ground with her front feet, standing her fur on end and showing her teeth. In this case, the predators would probably follow her – and the cheetah would escape due to her speed. The mother would behave in the same fashion if she were discovered as she led her cubs out into the open; by distracting the predators, the young might have the time to escape. But it does not always turn out well. A battle between a cheetah and other predators is generally a battle lost before it starts. Naturalists have long known that the greatest threat to cheetah cubs is other predators, and this is why mothers prefer to raise their young in zones where the other predators are less numerous, even if it means their prey is also less plentiful.

Cheetahs also suffer from another form of pressure exercised by other predators: having their kill stolen from under their noses. Hyenas have the habit of watching the comings and goings of a cheetah that lives on the same territory. As the cat has to rest for a full half jour or more after a chase, they can easily steal its prey. A female cheetah can do nothing when faced by even a single hyena. Unfortunately for her, lions and hyenas are not the only competitors for her food. Even male baboons will not hesitate to steal from her, and jackals and vultures are also able to chase her away from her meal. When researchers transmit the roar of a lion or yelp of a hyena to a cheetah, the feline moves away immediately, whether male or female. And after hearing such recordings, their success rate in hunting drops.

This clearly indicates that the pressure on cheetahs from other predators is substantial. The worry manifested by the cheetah is greater in the case of a lion's roar. Even where cheetahs are protected in national parks, they do not live well, due to the competition with other carnivores like lions and hyenas, which steal their kills and eat their young.

It appears that an ancestral hate exists between lions and leopards even though they hunt different prey. Lions generally attack larger prey than

138
A 14-month-old cheetah is hot on the heels of a jackal: excellent training for the chase! The yelping canine ends up hiding in the vegetation.

139
A leopard hesitates to leave the tree on which he has has spent the night since the hyenas below are searching for shreds of the carcass he let fall from the branches during his nighttime meal.

140-141 and 142-143
Three 14-month-old cheetahs and their mother are devouring a gazelle as a few vultures, attracted by the kill, land around them. A hungry vulture approaches one of the young cheetahs, which immediately charges it, just managing to escape its clutches. Finally, the cheetah, springing up on his back legs, attempts a final leap at the predatory bird.

leopards, having a clear size and strength advantage over other predators. Conscious of their vulnerability if surprised by a lion, leopards will abandon their kill and flee, otherwise they will drag their kills up a tree and take refuge.

If a lion has the chance to kill a leopard, it will do so without hesitation, even if it is not hungry. But then leopards kill lion cubs when they are found alone and defenseless. Of all the leopard's rivals, it is the hyena that steals its kills the most frequenty. Hyenas use their senses of hearing and smell to detect a leopard hunting and may be able to steal the leopard's prey before it succeeds in getting it up a tree. Hyenas kill many leopard cubs but rarely attack adults.

Faced by an individual hyena, the leopard may come off better, particularly if the leopard is a male, but when the hyenas arrive in a pack, the feline has no choice but to flee. Only large males may be able to put two hyenas to flight.

Another of the leopard's competitors – though only occasionally – is the crocodile, which sometimes leaves the river to steal the feline's prey. It has happened that crocodiles have killed and torn adult leopards to pieces after they ventured into the water.

The "match" between leopards and primates is very particular. The hostility of large monkeys toward leopards is constant. This is clear from watching the behavior of baboons, creatures that are so well organized and aggressive that they can cause serious problems to a leopard, even succeeding in killing it. Both leopards and baboons have fearsome canine teeth.

An adult male baboon weighs between 60 and 100 pounds, which is more than a female leopard. They are brave and dangerous adversaries, conscious of their ability to put a leopard to flight, especially a young female. By day baboons are able to chase a leopard away from its prey. The baboons in Leopard Gorge, for example, knew everything about Chui while she was raising her young and would often follow her. To escape the baboons, Chui would sometimes take refuge in a hole. Yves Christen (author of the book *Le Peuple Léopard*) once saw how a female leopard found herself trapped in a hole beneath a dead tree when chased by male chimpanzees in the tropical forest of the Ivory Coast. Protected in the hole, the leopard was almost safe but the chimpanzees made use of dried branches as sticks and gave her a few wallops. At each poke, the female leopard attacked her aggressors, attempting to bite their hands. After a couple of hours in these conditions, the chimpanzees made off and the leopard escaped. However, the balance of strength between baboons and leopards changes with nightfall. Settled on their perches for the night, the baboons make worried sounds, particularly if they hear a leopard cough. Leopards like to eat these primates, though it is not easy to catch them because they defend themselves as a community. But a wounded or isolated individual is fairly vulnerable.

144
Baboons run to steal a female cheetah's prey.

145
*Baboons charge a female cheetah that, in a previous
"encounter," had already lost a good piece of her tail.*

146-147
*Adolescent cheetahs, more reckless than their
mother, attack the hyena that hoped to rob the
family of their prey.*

147
*Every time she makes an early morning kill, hyenas
rob this female cheetah of her prey. She has to
change her strategy, hunting during the hotter hours
of the day, when her rivals rest.*

148 and 149
Lions are fearsome competition for cheetahs:
they steal their prey and kill their cubs whenever
they get a chance.

CHILDREN OF THE SAVANNA

150 left
Helpless children of the savanna: a six-week-old cheetah and a four-month-old leopard.

152
A female cheetah nurses her cubs in the ditch where she had hidden them. The little ones are born blind and begin to see when around ten days old.

153
A female cheetah carries her five-day-old cubs, one after the other, to a new hiding place: she must do this every two or three days to avoid an accumulation of their scent, which might attract hyenas or lions.

For several days we had been looking for Douma, whom we had seen mating four months earlier. It seemed she had chosen to live near the Tanzanian border. To animals the border is no obstacle, but for us it is: we cannot follow her into the Tanzanian section of the Serengeti Plain.

One morning we saw a female cheetah with swollen udders advancing toward us. It was not Douma but another female, Honey, whom we already knew. On seeing us, she behaved strangely: she hurried off, then stopped with her fur raised as she stroked her flanks with her tail. Evidently she was uncertain what to do. We decided to wait and not to move. This was a wise decision because, a few minutes later, Honey turned back and we heard high-pitched calls, rather like the chirping of a bird. Her cubs were calling her from a hollow in the midst of the tall grass. Honey lay down next to them, hidden to us by the grass, and stayed there all morning. Returning to the location at dawn the next day, we could make out five balls of fur at her side.

The cubs were still blind and weighed about half a pound each. They were only three or four days old. Their blackish and silvery coats were nothing like their mother's. After a little, Honey got up and went off to hunt, so we followed her at a distance. She ate quickly then abandoned the remains to return to her young. When we arrived the next day, the place was deserted. Honey had moved her cubs the previous evening or during the night. She could not have been far away but, as she was still lying on the ground, we could not see her in the long grass. We decided to wait until she stood up. An hour later her face appeared above the undergrowth. The family was about 450 yards from the previous lair where only trampled grass betrayed their passage as Honey had eaten her cubs' excrement. She cleaned them with her red tongue, which seemed very big compared to them, then suckled them.

Finally, she licked them again to help them relieve themselves. The days passed slowly; we couldn't see much because the youngsters remained almost completely hidden by the tall grass. In the middle of one afternoon, the mother looked around, sniffed the hiding place, paced a little around it, then picked up one of the cubs by the collar and carried it a hundred or so yards away. Then she returned to take the second and third. After three return trips, she lay down, but as the other two were calling her, she decided to return and take them. She then made a sixth journey and sniffed the previous hiding place to be sure she had not left any of her cubs behind. They were just beginning to be able to stand up, but they soon fell over.

Each day we noted the various stages of their growth and the movements that accompanied their development.

Their eyes opened at about 10 days and then they began to take a few uncertain steps.

The next day thirty or so buffalo passed close to the lair while Honey was hunting and only missed trampling them by a short distance. Three days later lions out hunting were headed in the direction of the cubs alone in the lair. We got the drivers of the safari jeeps to urge the lions discreetly but firmly away from the area. The cubs were safe – this time. But one morning we found only four. It seems that a lioness that lived nearby, a mother of equally small cubs, had killed one. The next day, Honey, who was very worried, moved the cubs four times.

One evening, when we had just left the mother with her young, using binoculars we made out the silhouette of another cheetah on a termite mound. It was Douma! Next to her were four cubs of five or six weeks, with a long silver mane down their backs. They already followed their mother everywhere so were quite visible to predators but too small to escape in case of trouble. This was the age in which they are at most danger!

The two mothers were less than a mile from one another. For us it was an extraordinary opportunity! For a number of weeks we followed either one or the other family, both of which remained in the same zone although the mothers took care to avoid one another. Honey's cubs grew rapidly and she had difficulty in carrying them in her mouth without hurting them when changing lair.

When their mother was away and it rained, the cubs huddled together in a large, shapeless ball. They didn't like the heavy downpours and called to their mother plaintively. When they were three weeks old, Honey's cubs started to take their first stumbling steps away from the lair, just a few yards, but each day they acquired more confidence. We watched them next to their mother, chasing after one another, as agile and graceful as kittens. Stretched out on her back, Honey allowed herself to be poked and bitten, occasionally calling them to order with a blow of her paw.

Douma's cubs loved to climb in the young acacia trees, their as yet unworn claws allowing them to indulge in gymnastics prohibited to adults. They often came to play around our vehicle and did not hesitate to lie on top of the tires. What perfect shade when the sun was hot! We were astounded by the many miles Douma sometimes made her cubs travel on a single day when searching for prey. We were able to follow them easily despite their tender age. Sitting on the hood of our car, one day Douma spied a prey. She gave out a short call to tell her cubs to keep quiet and set off on the hunt. But the disobedient cubs followed her, chasing after one another at the same time. It was an excellent way to spoil a hunt!

Douma was hungry and the family set off again. This time Douma made them obey her and the cubs lay down in the grass while their mother set off rapidly toward a small group of Thomson's gazelles. After killing a young antelope, she called her cubs and they trotted over on their little legs. As always, it was they that ate first. The gazelle was small and Douma had to hunt again to fill her own stomach. The next day she left her cubs again for several hours, then returned dragging the impala she had managed to bring down far from the lair.

A cub's day is mostly dedicated to play. They run, jump and ambush one another from behind rocks. One will creep up on a brother or sister, as it would do later while hunting, and take it by surprise. Douma was very patient with her playful cubs, which

would not hesitate to jump on her when she was lying down or walking. On one occasion, one of them stood up on its back legs and embraced her neck with its front ones and bit her. It is not easy to keep walking in such circumstances! Later the youngsters will begin to lose the black fur on their bellies and flanks and a part of their dorsal manes, and will thus increasingly resemble their mother.

Both Honey and Douma continually remained on the alert, studying their surroundings. They could not allow predators to approach too close as their cubs were not yet fast enough to be able to flee, but despite all her precautions Honey lost another youngster. As the family was walking through the bushes, two lionesses suddenly bounded out in front of them. Honey gave a cry of alarm and fled, followed by three of the cubs, but the unfortunate fourth cub got trapped by the lionesses. They knocked it this way and that, then threw it to the ground dead. From afar Honey called the missing cub to her with her strange birdlike chirp. She continued searching for it for several hours.

Following the growth of cheetah and leopard cubs is difficult during the first weeks because they all remain hidden, particularly the baby leopards. In October 2000, Zawadi gave birth to two cubs but we had no chance of seeing them. She set up a lair in Leopard Gorge. We tried to spy on them but it was impossible. During the first few days Zawadi spent as much time as possible with her cubs. She set out at nightfall to hunt, leaving them alone, but we did not hear them give any call. She would return during the night and warn them of her presence with a low rumble. We finally managed to surprise Zawadi as she was moving her cubs furtively to another cave at dawn. During the days that followed, she repeated

the operation several times, always choosing the hiding places her mother had used years before. Zawadi was scared of hyenas and lions, which were numerous in the area, as, eighteen months before, hyenas had killed her first litter, but these animals too use the same caves to give birth to their cubs. We had once seen a litter of hyenas just a few yards from where the two-week-old leopards were now.

The cubs were a male and female, which we named Millennium and Lisa. Zawadi made them return to their lair immediately. When they were about four weeks old, she took them out into the sunshine in front of their lair. She remained continually on the alert, her ears turning in all directions to hear even the minimum sound. Then she made them return inside before setting off for the hunt. They suffered her absence increasingly badly and we heard their shrill whining from inside the ravine. Zawadi returned and ordered them to be quiet with a dignified snort. During her absence they were supposed to remain absolutely silent. During the day even baboons could represent a lethal threat.

Over the following days we had the pleasure of seeing them come out. Their fur was much darker than their mother's and the groups of black spots closer together. Zawadi fussed over them tenderly. They continually tried to catch her long tail and squabbled together. Their mother encouraged them with a low call; it was not the growl heard when she was irritated, nor the snort she made when she wished to be left alone. When she had had enough, she went off a little distance but without ceasing to watch them and the surroundings.

Millennium and Lisa would play with plants and branches and roll together in the grass. They explored and sniffed everything around them and made a din.

Whatever moved attracted their attention. One morning they even hunted a frog and used a shrub to sharpen their claws and try climbing. One day a curious mongoose passed a little too close and the cubs chased it away growling. They already knew how to defend their territory! When the mother returned, they welcomed her by pressing their chests against her chin and rubbing themselves against her flanks. When they were two months old, Zawadi was still suckling them but began to bring them pieces of meat, which they used both for play and as a snack. They began to follow Zawadi at a distance among the rocks but very soon tired of this. They were just three months old when Zawadi took them with her to eat a kill for the first time. She had placed it on a fig plant that was very easy to climb. The baby leopards became increasingly adventurous and Lisa would sometimes crawl under our vehicle to gnaw at our tires. Millennium, however, was more timid.

A female cheetah that has had a successful encounter with a male or males will within three weeks or so search out a place to give birth, where her cubs will be hidden from view, for example, beneath a bush, in a dry riverbed or among the rocks.

At the start of the rainy season the litters are slightly more numerous, a fact that is undoubtedly linked to the increase in prey during this season, in particular the fawns of the Thomson's gazelles. Yet it is not possible to speak of a seasonal peak of births. The litters range from 2 to 6 cubs generally, though sometimes more; for example, Nanette, a female that lives in Nairobi National Park, is famous for being prolific. In 1993 she gave birth to 7 cubs. One disappeared before the age of 6 weeks and some weeks later Nanette abandoned another, which always remained behind; the rangers then discovered that it was suffering from a serious lung infection. The other 5 reached adulthood.

In her next litter, Nanette gave birth to 8 cubs. She lost 2 during the first few months, presumably to predators, but again she raised the others to the time they left her. Nanette, however, was an exception.

Newborn cubs weigh between roughly 0.5 and 1 pound at birth and increase at a daily rate of about 1.5 ounces at the start of their life. During the early weeks they have a sort of silvery-gray mane along their back.

It is assumed that this mane has different purposes: it serves as protection against the rain and sun and provides camouflage in the dry and burned grass; the color of the cub's fur and mane are also protective as it makes the cub resemble a ratel, a very aggressive African badger-like animal that frightens even leopards. The cubs keep this mane until about the age of two, though it gradually thins each month. Born blind, the cubs' eyes open at the start of the second week. During the first few days, the mother will move them from one hiding-place to another, carrying them one at a time by the scruff of the neck, to prevent predators from finding them from the scents that give away their presence and any traces left in the undergrowth.

Many young cheetahs do not survive the first few months, and it perhaps for this reason that litters of this species are more numerous that those of other

156
The beautiful silvery mane of these six-weeks-old cheetahs will disappear when they are about three months old and the normal mane appears.

157
Around four or five weeks old, cheetahs begin to follow their mother around the plains. They are not yet able to escape in the event of an attack: maybe this is why their fur makes them look like ratels, African badgers so aggressive they intimidate even lions.

157

large cats. Studies made in Serengeti Park showed that in the 1970s the litters numbered on average 5–6 cubs. In the 1980s zoologists noted that such large litters were rare so, worried by this state of affairs, they tried to find the causes. First, they wondered if the number of cubs was constant but that several were dying in the first few days, or whether the litters were really smaller, due perhaps to the lack of genetic diversity in the species. They demonstrated that young cheetahs are very vulnerable to predators and that in certain years only 5 percent live to maturity, at least in zones like the Serengeti and Masai-Mara, where there are many hyenas and lions. These two predators alone are responsible for the disappearance of 70 percent of cheetah cubs; only 30 pecent of cubs survive to the age in which they are able to trot after their mother, yet the mortality rate remains high in the two following weeks.

Another cause of death might be the mother abandoning her litter during the first weeks of their life; for example, in the Serengeti all it requires is for the Thomson's gazelles to leave the area where the mother has given birth for her to have to follow them, and therefore abandon her cubs. In certain years strong rains can also have dramatic consequences, with some litters being drowned in their den. Another danger is of being trapped by brushwood fires. A final risk is posed by male cheetahs: though no direct observations have been made of male cheetahs killing cubs, this hypothesis is not excluded but it seems to be very rare. Jonathan Scott, who has been observing leopards for many years, once saw a female fighting a male near the den in which she weaned her young on the day she lost her litter.

Cheetah cubs purr while they suckle. To stimulate the flow of the milk, they press on the mother's teats with their front paws. A weaning female has to eat more than usual to provide her with more energy, so she tries to bring down larger prey, such as adult gazelles, rather than make do with their young or with hares.

The mother continues to wean the cubs until the age of four months. When they leave their lair for the first time, around the age of 4 or 5 weeks, the mother follows them slowly, calling immediately to those that wander. When they are too small to run away quickly, they are in particular danger.

At this age they begin to eat solid food though they continue to suckle their mother as well. Between 3 and 6 weeks their milk teeth come through, and these last until the age of 8 months when they are replaced by their permanent set. Around 2 months, they begin to lose their black coat and much of their back mane. All that remains are a few long hairs on the nape. They become increasingly playful, running after one another on the plain and ambushing one another from behind tree trunks and rocks.

Play aids the cubs in acquiring their mother's reflexes. They learn to wait in ambush and to creep up without being seen. Their muscles, back, neck and legs all grow. To become a sprinter, a lot of training is needed! But when their mother goes hunting, they know they have to stop playing and stay almost completely still.

Female leopards also seek a quiet, shady place to give birth, one that is easy to defend, like the back of a cave. She has to take great care over her choice or other predators will profit from her mistakes. Leopard litters range from 1 to 6 cubs but the weakest die during the first hours of life. It is rare to see more

than two cubs come out into the open, and rarer still to see them live to adulthood. In the Masai-Mara Reserve, Jonathan Scott reports that he has never seen three cubs from the same litter reach the age of independence. Sometimes the mother will eat her dead cubs.

Newborn cubs are blind and weigh no more than 18 ounces, but they grow quickly. Their eyes remain closed for 6 to 10 days and they find their mother using their sense of smell. During the first days, the mother spends most of her time with her cubs. She keeps them warm and helps them to find her teats by lying on her side. When she has to hunt, she remains in the area and returns every few hours to suckle them and sometimes change their hiding-place.

When born, the cubs choose a teat and bathe it with their scent so that they can find it again easily. Each recognizes "his" or "her" teat before they even open their eyes and remains faithful to it. This way they can suckle together without squabbling and risking scratching their mother's skin in a tangle of paws. By licking the perineal region of the cubs' bodies, the mother stimulates them to urinate and defecate in the same way as the female cheetah does. Keeping them clean and warm helps to create the parental bond and is a very important task as rigorous hygiene is a guarantee of good health. The mother's saliva soothes grazes, keeps their fur in good condition (it easily gets dirty), and provides the cubs with vitamin D, the vitamin that, if in adequate supply, prevents rickets.

After a few days, the mother leaves the lair more often. Her cubs spend long periods alone, hidden but unprotected. Even if they are hungry they remain silent so as not to attract the attention of predators. Their mother returns invisible in the darkness. She alerts the cubs to her return with a sort of low growl that she uses later to put them on their guard if they wander too far off. Female tigers use the same sort of call but not lionesses or female cheetahs. This rumble is a very effective form of communication between the mother and her cubs; she has a series of sounds that she uses to communicate, mostly low in intensity so that only the cubs will hear them. When she arrives and her scent is recognized, the cubs call for her attention and to be suckled. Once they finish, they miaow and purr with satisfaction.

Female leopards leave their cubs hidden in the lair for the first 6 to 8 weeks of life even if the youngsters are able to walk a little after just a couple of weeks. And she leaves them for long periods of time, unlike her cheetah equivalent.

The mortality rate of leopard cubs is very high. Research shows rates of 50–60 percent in Mala Mala and Londolozi in southern Africa, and in the Masai-Mara it is even higher. Chui and Zawadi lost 4 in 5 of their cubs. Chui had 14, of which only 3 reached adulthood. Overall, at least half of all leopard cubs perish during their first year of life, of which two thirds die of hunger. The other principal cause of death is encounters with stronger predators. When her cubs die, the mother will mate again without delay. If she finds a dead cub, she will eat it. Is it possible that she does not recognize her own cubs? In any case, removing the carcasses reduces the risk of attracting other predators, like hyenas or lions, and may perhaps save any surviving members of the litter.

A very strong instinct impels even a mother leopard that has lost all her cubs to continue to call and search for them, using the same invitation she used to make them come out of the den and join her.

This practice persists for a week or more. The duration of the mother's search is justified by the fact that she often leaves her cubs alone for long periods, sometimes for several days when they are big enough, and therefore it is possible that they wander off from their hiding-place.

Female leopards can give birth at any time of the year though in some regions seasonal peaks exist. In Kruger National Park, for instance, there is a peak of matings at the end of the dry season when there is a strong concentration of impala. This leads to a peak in leopard births at the start of the wet season, which coincides with the birthing season of the impala. In contrast, in the Masai-Mara, the female leopards generally give birth during the long dry season and only seldom during the rainy season.

Female leopards move their young very frequently, almost every day during the first few weeks if they do not feel safe. The longer the cubs remain in one place, the higher the risk that they might be found and killed by a lion, hyenas or even a male leopard. Jackals, baboons, pythons and large eagles are also able to kill small felines if they are found without their mother. A martial eagle, which weighs up to 13 pounds and has a wingspan of up to 8'6", could kill and eat leopard cubs up to an age of 3 months. Leopards have a very particular smell and any passing lion or hyena would know unmistakably that a leopard had a lair nearby. When the mother begins to take her cubs out into the sunshine, they gradually get used to their new environment, though this will be limited to a few dozen yards around the den. They soon get their bearings in an area where their mother has left her scent around, then they gain confidence and explore a little farther away.

Leopard cubs spend a lot of time playing together or with their mother when she is present, but also with anything that they come across during their exploration of the "territory": grass, branches, elephant dung…. They investigate, sniff, scratch and make noise. To develop their muscles they try to climb small trees; at play they imitate the movements of their mother. These games develop their strength and teach them patience, and thus they gradually learn everything they will need during adult life.

Soon they are able to defend their territory against intruders and to torment the small animals that they find there. Before they reach even 8 weeks, they have tasted meat because their mother brings them scraps from large carcasses or small prey. They carefully observe the strongly smelling small animals. Then they start to play, jumping around the pieces of meat before sitting down to eat. It is the most astute that begins! But they are not able to feed well on meat as their little teeth cannot chew it. When there is only one cub, he has to manage all alone, like Beauty, whom we observed during the early months of her life. Some mothers take their cubs to eat the kills she has made from the age of 8 weeks, while others wait a little longer. When the cubs reach 3 or 4 months, the mother refuses to suckle them any longer, though they hardly weigh 7 pounds at that age.

If there is little prey about, weaning can be delayed, but once it occurs, the cubs follow their mother everywhere. The white patch on the tip of her tail allows them to keep an eye on her in the tall grass. She always gives them precedence when it comes to eating and will only take her turn when they are asleep beside her with their bellies full. From the moment in which the family moves around together, the cubs are very vulnerable and the mortality rate is extremely high.

160
Savuti moves her cubs from one hiding place to another, always bringing them to new crevices in the rocks.

161
Sometimes, in looking for food, the female cheetah will make her young travel several miles in a single day; they follow her without trouble despite their young age.

162
Young cheetahs stay hidden in the tall grass or in a ditch, barely visible, when their mother leaves to hunt. They are at the mercy of a number of threats: buffaloes, lions, hyenas….

163
At birth, the leopard weighs up to one pound, doubling its mass in four weeks and tripling it in six.

164-165
A young leopard's first venturing out: it accompanies its mother onto the pile of rocks selected for its hiding place, following her step by step.

On several occasions male leopards (generally those passing by and not the father) have been seen to kill cubs, for example, Chui gave birth to a new litter in 1997 in the Masai-Mara, and, one morning, a male leopard 3 years old entered the area where she had hidden her cubs. He was larger than Chui but less impressive than the resident male. He searched for the cubs nervously, often stopping to smell the rocks and following the trails of scent left by Chui. He entered a ravine to which the opening had been hidden by long grass and came out with a dead cub between his teeth. He went in again and came out with another trophy. Killing these cubs had a certain logic for him: they were the children of the resident male and, if they were killed, Chui would once more be in heat and accept the favors of other males. He therefore could hope to couple with her if the resident male had not already chased him away, but the territory was large and it was impossible to watch over it all.

Cheetah and leopard mothers not only have to ensure the survival of their cubs but also educate them. Raising the next generation to the age of independence is a difficult task because the mothers in these two species have to do everything alone. Males and females are only together during the mating period, then the female restarts her solitary life. Once she has become a mother she will not receive any help, either from males or other females. This is not the case with lionesses, which can take advantage of her pack's "nursery."

When a female cheetah or leopard goes hunting, she is obliged to leave her cubs unguarded, with all the risks that brings. She has to find prey not too distant from the lair, and this requirement limits her choice. If she does not find anything quickly, she may be away for 24 hours at a time, and this can only increase the risks to her cubs. When they begin to eat meat, the mother has not only to hunt for herself but for them too, therefore, the mother cheetah has to hunt each day instead of the every 2 or 3 days when she is alone.

She also has to kill more than once the same day as she always allows her cubs to eat first. This means that she hunts during the hot hours of the day, and this requires greater effort. And when the cubs leave the lair, she has to be on the lookout constantly so as not to allow predators to come close.

After just a few weeks, the females of the two species face different problems: it is easier for a female cheetah to find prey because her young are able to follow her sooner. The rapidity at which cheetah cubs achieve the capability to move around is commensurate to the size of the mother's domain and this allows her to hunt those prey that are more easily available. This is vitally important in the Serengeti and certain sections of the Masai-Mara where the main prey is the Thomson's gazelle – a migratory species. It is not uncommon for mothers to abandon their litter if they are unable to follow her when it is necessary to hunt a long way off: with a gestation period of only 3 months, it is more "productive" to start a new pregnancy when the conditions are more favorable.

On the other hand, cheetah cubs are highly visible to predators and their mother must be very watchful. Certain female cheetahs are better mothers than others, and some never succeed in bringing their young to adulthood.

A female leopard with cubs is obliged to be more active in daytime, so the risk she faces is even greater.

166-167
*This leopard only five month old has a brother,
but no longer spends all its time with him: as it
sleeps on a trunk, the other one (not seen in the
photo) rests not far away, under a bush.*

167
*As night falls a young leopard follows its mother
up the tree where she has placed her kill. At two
months old, a cub begins to be able to follow his
mother anywhere, feeding on a combination of
meat and milk.*

168

Just before gaining her independence, this young female leopard often plays with her mother, but within a few months they will avoid each other: in the event of a meeting, the mother will in fact drive her off as she will have become competition.

169

A small leopard plays with its mother, which protects it tenderly between her paws. The female leopard rarely raises more than one or two cubs at a time; therefore, she is often her offspring's only playmate.

170 and 171
Even though the female leopard spends as much time as possible with her young, she is forced to leave them alone to hunt and patrol her territory. When this occurs, the cubs stay hidden and silent, going out only in their mother's company.

172-173
Back from the hunt, the female leopard calls her
two-month-old little ones with a low growl,
which she uses also to warn them when they
wander off too far.

173
When female leopards have more than one cub,
each chooses a nipple and marks it with its own
scent. In this way, the little ones – which will be
weaned at about three months old – do not fight
among themselves and do not scratch their
mother.

174

174, 175, and 176-177
At 15 days old, with their eyes having only
recently opened, cheetahs manage to take a few
steps, but they get tired quickly: hence, they go
to their mother to suckle and be licked.

178-179 and 179
Day after day, the little cheetahs gain
confidence, scuffling like kittens. Playing, they

mostly run and, unlike lions, fight little. This
pattern reflects the importance of speed in
hunting for cheetahs; lions are not great runners
but have the strength to kill large prey.

180 and 181
Young cheetahs love climbing small acacia trees;
their claws, not yet blunted, allow them to
perform acrobatics impossible for adults.

182 and 183
*Female cheetahs not only put up with the antics
of their young, they actually take part – though
they do have to calm them down every now and
then with a swat of their paw.*

184 and 185
*Lounging on her back, this female cheetah
allows herself to be attacked by her little one, the
only one of the litter to have survived: for a
playmate, there is only mommy.*

186 and 187
Female cheetahs do not join forces to raise their offspring as lionesses do. Furthermore, the males stay only long enough to mate, so a mother's job is truly hard.

188 and 189
On a torrid afternoon, a female cheetah and her cubs have stopped on open ground, where night will overtake them. In the early morning, they will still be there, curled up one against the other.

YOUNG FELINES

190 left
Bella and her male cub at six months old.

190 right
Two adolescent cheetahs, around 14 months old, have caught a small Thomson's gazelle on their own.

192
Unaware of the caution crucial to life in the savanna, six-month-old cheetahs chase each other on open ground. As long as their mother continues to hunt for them, the young felines will behave carelessly.

193
A female cheetah makes a young antelope its lose balance, which then, dragged down by the momentum, somersaults onto its back. The cat tightens its jaws around its throat but without killing it: first she will bring it to her cubs.

D
ouma and her cubs cover large distances in the plains where for us there are few reference points. To have any chance of finding our cheetah family in the morning, every evening we have to record their position in the middle of nowhere using our GPS (global positioning satellite) and return there the next morning before they set out. Fortunately for us, they rarely move at night unless they are disturbed by hyenas or lions. We often find them still asleep 2 or 3 yards from our signal. But we often have to search for them, describing circles around our recorded position. Sometimes, to find them again, we have to wait until one of them stands up in the grass. When crouching against one another in the grass, they are practically invisible.

At four months, the cheetah cubs –"the Daltons" as we nicknamed them – start playing silly games. They run, chase one another, jump up onto termite mounds and tree trunks, even when Douma wants to hunt. Fortunately, she is a particularly skilled hunter and so succeeds in making her kills anyway. Some Thomson's gazelles have given birth and Douma takes advantage of the situation to teach her cubs how to hunt. Having caught a fawn, rather than suffocate it as usual, she carries it live to them in her teeth and places it next to them. The little ones stare at the gazelle immobile, in a state of shock. They don't know what to do with this strange "toy."

The fawn stays still for a few moments then, having recovered a little of its strength, starts running. The cubs react, and play with it, making it part of one of their many games. They follow it and immobilize it with their paws. Douma watches without intervening. Within an hour the cubs are tired and end by ignoring the baby gazelle, which runs off. Then Douma decides to take a hand and kills it. Her cubs are still incapable of doing so. Then she leaves them to eat their tiny victim.

In the days that follow, no other fawn is born but, a week later, Douma restarts her hunting lessons with the cubs. This time they are more at ease with their prey and soon trap it to the ground. But then they start running round like mad again. They are still very young and have several months ahead to learn to hunt.

The weeks pass and the Daltons are in fine form. They have become more active during hunts and run behind their mother when she hurls herself into the chase, but they are still very far from being as fast as she is. One day, one of the male cubs is bitten by a puff adder and dies rapidly. Douma and the rest of the cubs remain a long time by the body. Even while it is raining three days later, Douma continues calling as though he were not dead. Then all four change their zone to follow the movements of the gazelles.

When September arrives the two surviving males and female are almost as big as their mother. Many Thomson's gazelles have given birth. Every mother eats her placenta, cleans the fawn and moves it a few yards so as not to leave scents that may attract predators. The newborn fawn remains hidden in the brush, its coat helping to camouflage it. If there are no scents to help them, the cheetahs and hyenas wander through the tall grass in search of young

gazelles born during the night. Douma and her cubs find more than one on some mornings.

Now the Daltons are able to suffocate these fawns themselves. One morning a jackal approaches too close to the cubs and they chase after it at an incredible speed. They torment the howling beast ceaselessly, and it ends up by taking shelter in a bush, but even then the cubs do not let up. All this time Douma watches the hunt though without personal interest as cheetahs do not eat jackals. She then starts looking for fawns again but keeps an eye on her youngsters. In the end they turn back to her exuberant.

For a number of weeks the baby gazelles are easy prey to the cheetahs, but this does not prevent the Daltons from running after zebras and gnu, though without the minimum chance of bringing them down. One afternoon the young female decides to give chase to a small warthog. She sprints off, followed by her brothers, but the warthog's mother charges them to save her young – and the female cheetah is forced to run away. Then the Daltons start their games again; this time the two males simulate coupling with their sister.

During the time that has passed they have not learned much about hunting; they continue to let themselves be seen by their prey while Douma is creeping up, or to fling themselves into the chase from too far away.

But the skilful Douma is sometimes able to profit from their clumsiness. One morning she spied some male gazelles. Her cubs continued to play well in sight of two of the antelopes, which kept a beady eye on them without fleeing as they felt safe from the three cheetahs. Douma, on the other hand, kept herself at some distance from the cubs and was hidden in the grass. She crept up on the gazelles slowly without letting herself be seen as we watched her progress with binoculars. The two males had no idea of her presence and Douma reached the ideal distance for a burst of speed. After a short chase she killed one of the males and the Daltons had only to turn up to share the meal.

Finally, one day in October, Douma killed a female impala and left her cubs to eat, then wandered off. The Daltons ate without thinking about her, then slunk off to the shade to sleep after the big meal. But Douma did not return. All afternoon and for the next three days the bewildered cubs called for her, then the young female took the initiative and went hunting but she started her charge too far away. Fortunately the next morning the cubs found two fawns so they were able to feed.

Now brothers and sister had to hunt together. After a few months, the young female left her brothers to begin her life as a solitary female.

We then went to watch the leopard Bella and her cubs of approximately five months. The small male leopard was sleeping in a bush, only just visible, and his sister was stretched out a little way off. Bella returned to them in the evening and led them up a tree where she had laid out the carcass of a freshly killed impala. The first to arrive was the male, who was already bigger than his sister. Taking advantage of this, he prevented her from eating, snarling at her and bringing out his claws. Soon he was full and it was her turn to eat.

The next morning at dawn we found them playing in the grass, then they climbed the tree once more. Sometimes they were clumsy and had even fallen to the ground a few days earlier as they pulled up a small animal over which they had been arguing feverishly. Bella watched without intervening as no danger threatened.

The young male climbed up with the carcass in his jaws. It was not easy for us to follow this family because it seemed that Bella deliberately crossed from one side of the River Talek to the other. The banks were covered with dense bushes and there were only two fords that allowed vehicles to cross, and as soon as we reached one, she would hide herself again in the vegetation preventing us from finding her.

As for Zawadi and Lisa, they had gone to an area that was very difficult to enter, nonetheless, we sometimes managed to spot her. That day, late in the afternoon, Lisa, who was now almost a year old, headed toward a small rocky canyon. When she was a few hundred yards away she froze and listened to the noises coming from the rocks. Suddenly, she hurled herself on a hyrax and carried it in her mouth for a few yards.

When she put it down, it began to scamper off crying: Lisa had not killed it. She jumped on it again and held it in her claws. The hyrax escaped again and Lisa caught it once more. The game lasted half an hour until Lisa killed it by breaking its backbone above the shoulders. Having eaten only a few hours earlier from the carcass of an antelope killed by her mother Zawadi, she was not very hungry and had used the hyrax to play. At this point Lisa lay down

beneath a bush alone. She did not go close to Zawadi, who slept a short distance away in a tree.

At nightfall the next day, the two females met up and greeted each other by rubbing faces, thenthey played together like overgrown kittens. Zawadi seemed pleased to see her daughter. As the weeks passed, the two saw one another less often and Lisa hunted small prey alone for nourishment. When we found Lisa again a few months later, she was alone. We followed her for four days without seeing her mother. On the fifth day, Zawadi found herself in the same zone as her daughter, but when Lisa came to greet her mother, Zawadi showed her teeth and made off. She behaved as though she had left this part of her territory to her daughter. Fifteen days earlier she had been seen with a large male in Leopard Gorge, and we hoped that she had become pregnant once more.

Lisa had no playmates from the age of 4 months when her brother was killed by a lioness. Years before, Mong'aa and Taratibu gave us the opportunity to watch them play their numerous games, including those of adolescence. And they left us a particularly lovely memory: one evening Michel had just finished cooking pork chops in the camp a little over a mile from the gorge. Suddenly he saw two not so very large leopards but climbed in the vehicle as a precaution. He recognized Mong'aa and Taratibu, adolescents of 14 months at the time. Although they were not as big as an adult leopard, they could certainly kill a man, especially the powerful male. Michel sat inside our vehicle for almost an hour, watching them eat his meat, rip the napkins to shreds and play with the saucepan. They

continued to play close to him and remained for several hours. It was a powerful and unforgettable experience.

The young of both the cheetah and leopard species are weaned at 3 or 4 months. At first the mother refuses to let their cubs suckle but nevertheless they succeed in drinking a little milk for a few days more. If the cubs insist on suckling, the mother will show her teeth and snarl. Once weaning is complete, there is no longer any peaceful living between brothers and sisters. They chase one another away from carcasses, growl, spit, rumble and scratch, and are capable of brawls of a violence that does not occur among lions and cheetahs from the same litter. Sometimes the mother has to intervene to calm things down. She separates her cubs, biting the adversaries equally, and will occasionally take the carcass away. Each cub has to learn to repress violent behavior toward the others. Besides performing a conciliatory role to prevent her cubs from injuring one another, the mother also worries about the noise created by such brawls, afraid they might attract the attention of predators. When there are only two in a litter, one becomes the dominant partner, either because it is a male and thus is larger and stronger than a female, or simply because it has a more combative temperament than the other.

Cheetahs do not fight one another over prey and share the food without argument. Cheetahs are unable to carry a kill to safety in a tree. This is detrimental: if each waits to take his turn, then they have to eat in a hurry before the vultures attract the lions or hyenas.

Cheetah cubs have difficulty in recognizing predators even after they reach 4 months of age (when they are able to flee) and thus are slow to react. It is therefore the mother's task to identify predators from a distance and prevent them from coming close, for example, by deciding to move away from the area. Her vigilance is at its greatest from when the cubs begin to follow her until weaning, after which time it gradually diminishes. Yet the cubs are still unable to identify potential dangers until they are 10 months old or so.

The education of young leopards is very different; they sent a surprising amount of time alone, unlike young cheetahs, which are always with their mother. A leopard cub does not seem to suffer when separated from its companions (a young lion or cheetah will give out desolate cries). Leopards very soon get used to exploring their environment alone, often finding themselves separated from their mother and even their brothers and sisters.

When a cub is awaiting its mother, it simply takes shelter in a hollow, beneath a bush or in a tree. The mother will call her cubs to tell them of her arrival and to greet once more. This independency increases month by month. When they sleep or rest, brothers and sisters choose separate places, preferring to remain alone rather than together. As they grow, a mother no longer searches for her cubs when she returns, it is for them to find her. During the early part of their life, young leopards play together for hours and many of their games imitate behavior that they must know at the moment they leave to live their own lives: to lie in ambush, to bite in the way their mother does to kill her prey, to flee from an attack, etc.

The games that cheetahs play have more to do with racing and chasing, as in a hunt, and less to do

with fighting – the opposite of how lion cubs behave. This particular difference is due to the enormous importance that speed plays in the cheetah's hunting technique as compared to the short sprints made by lions. With their claws still sharp and more extendible than those of adults, the young cheetahs can climb easily in trees, where they love to play, but soon their claws become blunt and they are no longer able to do so.

Young leopards do not follow their mother when she goes hunting and so are unable to watch her in action. This is because she has to remain hidden to get as close as possible to the victim as possible. But the mother often brings back small prey still alive to her cubs so that she can show them how to kill it with a bite. Later the cubs will follow her example with small prey like birds and lizards.

It is difficult to know at what age a leopard can kill his first small mammal autonomously. It seems that in general it occurs between 6 and 9 months of age but everything depends on circumstance and their skills. Jonathan Scott saw Zawadi's daughter kill a hyrax around the age of 3 months. With regard to larger prey, Beauty was able to kill adult Thomson's gazelles at the age of a year. Young males, which are stronger and larger than their sisters of the same age, manage to catch prey larger than themselves. In southern Africa, Hess (who's he??) saw an 11-month-old male kill a young male impala by suffocating it in the same manner as an expert adult. In the Phinda Reserve in Natal, 7-month-old cubs managed to survive after the death of their mother.

In Ngala in Kruger National Park, two cubs hardly 3 months old succeeded in killing their first antelope though It was a small one. But the perpetrators of these exploits were particularly skilled or favored by fortune.

Young cheetahs watch their mother carefully as she hunts even if they long remain a hindrance to her. Placing fawns in front of them, she gives them a real hunting apprenticeship, but the cubs are unable to suffocate their prey as an adult does until they are 10 months old.

Apprenticeship usually begins at the age of 5 or 6 months but depends on the availability of suitable prey. During their education, they must learn which are the right animals to hunt, and for a long time they will give chase to jackals, zebras, gnus and even giraffes! Some were even seen amusing themselves bothering a male lion at rest! They experience many failures before learning to choose the right moment to shoot off after their prey and to learn how to get close without being seen.

The more the cubs grow, the greater their need for meat despite their being unable to contribute to obtaining it in a significant way. Yet studies in the Serengeti show that mothers do not try to hunt larger prey, consequently, they eat less than solitary females and cover greater distances. But experts have not observed that they were hungry. It is only when the cubs enter adolescence that, if the litter is a large one, the mothers try to bring down larger prey. As their youngsters grow, they are able to lower their guard a little with respect to predators, as these tend to avoid families with adolescent cubs.

At one year old a young male leopard has all his permanent teeth even if the canines have not reached their full size. This occurs between the ages of 18 and 24 months and is important for him to be able to kill larger prey.

The transition to independence happens gradually. The young leopard, accustomed to being alone, refines his hunting techniques. Relations with his mother will cool progressively until a state of hostility is reached. The mother does not welcome the youngster's approach and responds by showing her teeth and growling. She shows that she wants to be left alone and that the young male has to look after himself. She has already ceased to lead him to her own kills though she will not chase him away when he arrives on the scene.

Most leopards become independent at the age of one or two years. The possible period is fairly wide because the stronger young males leave at between 12 and 16 months, whereas their sisters stay for a few months more. Males begin to spend time away even at the age of a year but returning every so often until they make the break complete.

The birth of a new litter may be the decisive in instigating the separation and will change the mother's behavior. It often happens that a female leopard gets pregnant before her adolescent cubs have gone their own ways. On average, the gap between pregnancies for a leopard is 18 to 24 months, though of course there are exceptions. The closer the female is to the birth, the more she tries to stay hidden and alone. This behavior contributes to the severing of the remaining links.

The birth of new cubs, however, does not automatically imply separation from the previous litter, for example, Chui mated when Beauty was only 10 months old and 3 months later produced her fourth litter. At that time Beauty was already able to catch small prey she found in the bushes, such as hares and young impala, but she was not yet able to survive alone. In the months that followed, she

continued to eat the kills that Chui made and was seen several times playing with her new brothers and sisters. Chui let her do so, growling when she wanted Beauty to move away or when the games between the cubs and the adolescent leopard got too rough. Later on, Beauty was seen allowing a little brother and sister to eat one of her kills.

The first phase of independent life is difficult. The leopards at that stage are not skilful at hunting and do not have their own territory. They may require 2 years of apprenticeship. Often they hunt cercopithecus monkeys in the trees, something an adult would be too dignified to do. A young male in Mala Mala Game Reserve in South Africa was observed trying to kill giraffes, adult kudus, gnus and even tried it on with a herd of buffaloes, but they charged him and forced him to take shelter up the nearest tree.

The path to independence is lined with lethal traps for sub-adult leopards (between 18 and 42 months), especially the males which have to conquer their own territory. Their mortality rate is practically double that of adult leopards. If the ratio between males and females at birth is roughly 1:1, it falls to about 1:2 as adults. In the Masai-Mara, Serengeti and Kruger protected areas, the best hunting territories are already taken and defended by resident males that are stronger than the sub-adults. Therefore the younger animals either have to fight a resident or to live in a zone where it is difficult to hunt and mate. Like wounded adults and old leopards, the youngsters may find themselves having to attack livestock or dogs to survive, but in so doing risk being trapped or poisoned by man.

A young male that has only just made the break remains close to his mother to begin with, hunting on

her territory, though this may also belong to his father. When he becomes a potential rival for the resident males, the youngster has to leave, sometimes having to travel far away. Young females, as we have seen, continue to live on a section of their mother's territory, or on the edge of it. But this arrangement does not work out when there is not enough living space for everyone, in particular when a female succeeds in raising several daughters to independence.

Then the new adults are obliged to take off and battle for their own territories, even if it is with a "relative." This is what happened to Chui's mother, who had to travel far from her birthplace.

The mother cheetah behaves very differently with her adolescent children than the mother leopard does. There is no gradual separation, nor a progressive loosening of family ties; the mother does not drive her youngsters away when they rub against her or eat her kills. The break is a sudden and harsh one and can occur without any particular preconditions. It generally takes place when the young are between 15 and 18 months old. As soon as they reach sexual maturity (about 16–18 months), some young males actually court their own mother. It is very rare for a family to come back in contact after the break has been made but, if it happens, the mother and her children ignore one another, all the more so as the mother does not defend her domain. The break is generally instigated by the mother, who has more to gain by abandoning her adolescent children than remaining with them, at least from the standpoint of feeding.

In any case, she has to separate from them to give birth to a new litter as she would not be able to hunt for them and accumulate sufficient reserves to suckle a younger generation.

Brothers and sisters remain together for 6 or 7 months after leaving their mother, hunting together and sharing their kills, then the females leave to live alone. They will have their first litter at around the age of three. Adolescents of both sexes suffer from the break with their mother.

They are often hungry as they are not skilled hunters: experience comes with age. The youngsters attack many "wrong" prey, herbivores spy them approaching more often than they do adults, and in general they set off on the chase from too far away.

Once young males have reached independence, they are obliged to spend more time hunting as, until then, they had let their mother and sister(s) do the work. In fact, it is often the female cheetahs that take the initiative and the males remain idle or mount a rear guard without expending much effort. In consequence, it is not the males that initiate the break. Often it is the young females that are ready to leave the family first.

The young males that have been forced to leave their mother too soon try to join another family or even a group of males, sharing the kills made by the foster-mother or the males, or stealing it. Behavior of this kind keeps them alive; in spite of the aggressiveness of the female, this type of solution may last several months. This explains the confusion that has arisen over the composition and size of groups of cheetahs, especially as from a distance adolescents look like adults. At the moment of the separation, the young females may be as large as their mother and the young males even more so. It is for this reason that some observers have recorded groups of ten or more adults! Something that seems quite impossible.

208 and 209
Young cheetahs are particularly active in the
early morning. They run, sprint, and set
themselves up in ambush behind a rock or
termite hill: one of them approaches its
companions without being seen, as it will do
later with prey, and takes them by surprise.

210 and 211
A six-month-old cheetah has finally managed to
climb up a vertical tree trunk. However, his
brother, for fun, tries to pull him down.

212 and 213
*Unlike the fighting that goes on between young
leopards, by nature more solitary and competitive,
the fighting between these two adolescent male
cheetahs is only for fun: aggressive behavior does
not occur between them.*

214 and 215
A small warthog flees from the cheetahs. At first,
the mother of the piglet does nothing aggressive,
but when one of the young felines is about to catch
it, she intervenes, charging the cats. The cheetah
calculated the risks badly and has to escape.

216, 217, and 218-219
A cheetah has brought her four-month-old
young, at the age when they learn to hunt, a
small live gazelle. However, the cubs do not
understand and start to play with the new
arrival. The mother watches without
intervening, and only when the victim tries to
get away will she kill it.

220
A five-month-old leopard warms himself
in the morning sun: dawn, in Masai-Mara,
is always cold.

P H O T O G R A P H I C
C R E D I T S

Photos by Christine and Michel Denis-Huot,
except for the following:
14 Araldo De Luca/Archivio White Star; 15 Christie's
Images/Corbis/Contrasto; 16 Academy of Natural Sciences
of Philadelphia/Corbis/Contrasto; 17 Christie's
Images/Corbis/Contrasto; 18 Mary Evans Picture Library;
19 top Roger Viollet/Archivio Alinari; 19 bottom Bridgeman
Art Library/Archivio Alinari; 20 Archivio Scala;
21 Bridgeman Art Library/Archivio Alinari; 22 top
Bridgeman Art Library/Archivio Alinari; 22 bottom
Bridgeman Art Library/Archivio Alinari; 23 Bridgeman Art
Library/Archivio Alinari; 24 ICP/DOUBLE'S; 25 top
ICP/DOUBLE'S; 25 bottom Archivio Scala; 26 J.G Berizzi/
Photo RMN; 27 Bridgeman Art Library/Archivio Alinari

Great thanks go to the felines of the African savanna, with whom we have lived for many years,
and to all the women and men that work to protect nature and the wild animals in Kenya and Tanzania.
Christine and Michel Denis-Huot

The photographs in this book were taken with Canon equipment:
the EOS-1V camera body for shots on film, the EOS-1D and EOS-Mark II for digital pictures;
lenses were from 16-35 to 600 mm.

The traditional photographs were taken with Fuji, Sensia, and Provia film.